Mike R.,

Thank you for helping me with this book. You have been such an inspiration for me, and for so many in the program. Our journeys through this world are filled with trials and joys. Going through this life in recovery with you has surely been one of my joys.

Blessings and peace always,
Rich H.

P.S.
You are a great example of the true meaning of transformation through sobriety: of striving to be the best people we can be for God, our families + friends and ourselves. That's so much more than not drinking!

Thanks, again,
Rich

What People Have to Say about *Under Construction*

"An inspired, incredibly insightful and practical guide to personal and spiritual growth in recovery. The wisdom and understanding Rick acquired through years of seeking and practicing spiritual principles on a daily basis is poured out in this work of love. He cogently lays out tools of recovery, succinctly explains how these tools can be used in our daily lives, and then beautifully illustrates the awesome benefits we receive as we use these tools and apply these principles throughout our lives."
-Bill K. Sobriety date, January 18, 1984

"Rick's recovery tools could just as well be translated into how to live a life worth living. Simple but profound truths or should I say precious gems, that if applied, will lead a person out of a life of hopelessness and despair into a life of hope, love and peace. I wouldn't hesitate to recommend this book to my clients."
-Dan Bero MA, LCPC. A licensed psychotherapist in private practice for 27 years

"For years I was Rick's pastor. We became good friends when we co-founded a Spiritual Breakfast that met every month for five years. Most participants were in recovery from addiction to alcohol, but not all. Dealing with spiritual issues struck a chord; participation grew. Eventually we added annual and then biannual weekend spiritual retreats. We recently completed our thirteenth retreat with record attendance. Rick has identified and compiled practical, tried and tested tools to bring life-changing health to people in recovery. Seeing how effectively God worked in the lives of those who came to our breakfasts and retreats brought strength and joy to my own faith. Rick walks the talk. His tools come out of his real-life experience. They work. This superbly written book is full of powerful tools that will equip those who read it with what it takes to experience a full and blessed life. I highly recommend it."
-Rev. Gates Vrooman, D. Min.

"Twenty-five insightful tools to guide anyone choosing to recover from an addiction. Presented in an easy to understand manner with helpful examples & thought provoking questions. This book would be useful in a recovery study group as well as for individual self-examination."
-Mary Beth H. Sobriety date, August 5, 2002

"The tools presented in Rick's book can turn your life around – if you have the guts to follow it, a pragmatic book that will give you insight to the triggers that can accelerate progress in recovery and all relationships. Prepare for tough-hitting questions and no-holds-barred action steps. The book goes straight to tackling the biggest challenges facing anyone in recovery and should be a standard resource for all who participate or work in a recovery program."
-Todd S. Sobriety date, October 24, 2011

"The compelling tools and beliefs in this work are uniquely notable due to the author's own experience and recovery. It is based on what truly makes a difference, not some theory, idealistic essay, or abstract endeavor. Most of all, it is a far-reaching account to be read and applied. Application of these principles can lead to implementing methods and ways for effective daily living. It is a must read book for anyone looking for recovery from addiction."
-Joe B. Sobriety date, March 7, 1970

"Individuals who are recovering from alcohol dependence, or any other type of substance dependence, need several different types of support and guidance. Rick H. offers two different types of help--inspiration and encouragement on one level, and many highly practical tips on another level. Over and over again, individuals in recovery, their family members, and the professionals who assist them will see clearly that the wisdom in this short book is authentic and was hard-earned."
-Dr. Jim Clopton, Licensed Psychologist

Under Construction

25 Life-Building Tools for
Addicts in Recovery

Rick H.

WestBow
PRESS
A DIVISION OF THOMAS NELSON

WestBow Press books may be ordered through booksellers or by contacting:

WestBow Press
A Division of Thomas Nelson
1663 Liberty Drive
Bloomington, IN 47403
www.westbowpress.com
1-(866) 928-1240

Books may also be ordered through author's website.

Because of the dynamic nature of the Internet, any web addresses or links contained in
this book may have changed since publication and may no longer be valid. The views
expressed in this work are solely those of the author and do not necessarily reflect the
views of the publisher, and the publisher hereby disclaims any responsibility for them.

Any people depicted in stock imagery provided by Thinkstock are models,
and such images are being used for illustrative purposes only.

Certain stock imagery © Thinkstock.

ISBN: 978-1-4497-6700-6 (e)
ISBN: 978-1-4497-6701-3 (sc)
ISBN: 978-1-4497-6702-0 (hc)

Library of Congress Control Number: 2012916634

Printed in the United States of America

WestBow Press rev. date: 12/6/2012

Dedication

THIS BOOK IS DEDICATED to all my fellow travelers who, although their roads were burdened with the struggle of active addiction, have come out on the other side: where there is light and hope for a wonderful future. For without our fellowship, I would be alone and lost.

A special thanks to my sponsors Gary M., Lenny C., and Joe B., and my spiritual adviser, Pastor Gates Vrooman, who have guided me over the years on my spiritual journey of recovery.

To my wife Sue, my daughter Stephanie, and my son Scott: thanks for your love, kindness, and acceptance as we grew up as a family, through the bad and good times.

Foreword

S OMEONE HAS SAID, "WHEN the student is ready, the teacher
will appear." If you are reading these words, you now may be
ready to encounter a teacher with incredible practical knowledge in
how to deal successfully with addiction and how to experience a full
and rewarding life.

Rick and I met when he and his family first visited the church
where I was serving as senior pastor in a Chicago suburb. When he
and his family came forward for Communion, he refused to take
the little cup of grape juice. I offered it several times, but he clearly
shook his head "no." Yet he took the bread. His family took both
the bread and the cup.

"That's really odd," I thought. "What's with this guy?"

After the worship service, he came up to me with a warm yet bashful smile and said, "You must be wondering what was going on with me at Communion."

"Well," I started to say.

He took a step closer. "I didn't mean to catch you off guard," he said. "I'm in recovery. I've been sober since April of 1990 and I just don't want to take any chances by drinking the wine."

"Wine? We don't serve wine at Communion," I said. "We serve grape juice." I'm sure my face registered a look of astonishment.

Rick looked down at his shoes and, with a slight smile, softly said, "I didn't know."

"We've never served wine," I said, not wanting to sound defensive. Then I paused. "But how would you have known that."

Sue, his wife, in a very pleasant tone suggested, "Perhaps something could be said in the bulletin where you print directions about Communion."

"That's a good idea," I said. And from then on, every time we celebrated Communion, the bulletin carried a statement indicating that we serve non-alcoholic grape juice.

In that first meeting, Rick became my teacher and made me more sensitive to persons who are in recovery. Although I am not an alcoholic, I was a student ready to learn. He sensed my interest and invited me to an open AA meeting where he was scheduled to give the lead. Sue and another couple offered to sit with me if I wanted to go. I did and thus began a deep and meaningful friendship. It was a joy to serve as a pastor to Rick and his family and to others in recovery who came to worship at our church.

Our friendship grew deeper when Rick and I co-founded a Spiritual Breakfast that met every month for five years. Most participants, but not all, were in recovery from addiction to alcohol. Dealing with spiritual issues struck a chord; participation grew. Eventually we added annual and then biannual weekend spiritual retreats. We recently completed our 13th with record attendance.

Over the years, Rick sensed that God was calling him to do something else once he left the hectic corporate world. I agreed, and I encouraged him to use his personal gifts and experiences for some worthy purpose. At that time, he wasn't clear what, exactly, God was calling him to do. But it had to be something more than daily rounds of golf! It wasn't clear back then, but now it is: write a book to help addicts in recovery.

Rick has identified and compiled practical, tried and tested tools to bring life-changing health to people in recovery. Seeing how effectively God worked in the lives of those who came to our breakfasts and retreats brought strength and joy to my own faith. Rick walks the talk. The 25 tools come out of his real-life experience. They work. This superbly written book is full of powerful tools that will equip those who read it with what it takes to experience a deeply satisfying and blessed life.

Under Construction, 25 Life-Building Tools for Addicts in Recovery is not merely a book to read and lay aside. It is a book we will want to return to, time and again. In this book, Rick prompts us to think, question and gain insights into our own lives. He helps us connect to a Power greater than ourselves. His real-life stories engage us; they speak to our real lives. He has definitely walked in our shoes. His questions help us get to the root of the matter and lead us to personal growth. His choice of quotes help us nail down the wisdom and learning in each tool. Rick deals with the deep things of life, especially spirituality; at the same time, his writing style is easy to understand and apply to our own lives. I highly recommend *Under Construction, 25 Life-Building Tools for Addicts in Recovery.*

Rev. Gates Vrooman, D.Min.

Contents

Preface

WHY DID I WRITE this book? First, more and more I seek to do the will of God as I have come to understand it. Some time ago, after my job in corporate America was eliminated and I stopped working, I was asked often what I was going to do for this season in my life. After a period of physical and emotional recovery, only one thing came to mind (repeatedly): I must write a book that presents, in a clear and concise manner, tools of recovery that have transformed my life and those of millions of others suffering from addictions.

The "spiritual nudge" to write this book was not a major surprise, since I love to write and had written numerous articles on my journey in recovery, which were published by several recovery periodicals. After rereading these articles, two themes became evident: first, I have learned and adopted many powerful life tools that have aided me in my 22 years of freedom from alcohol addiction; second, many of these tools are spiritually based, which I believe coincides with the spiritual prompting to write this book.

While reading and writing articles on recovery and attending a variety of addiction recovery groups, a realization emerged in a clear and powerful way: although my particular addiction is to alcohol, *the tools of recovery that aid in maintaining physical and emotional sobriety are fundamentally relevant to recovery from all addictions.* The basis of this lies in the core nature of addiction itself: people chained to addictive patterns are attempting to escape from themselves, from their inability to effectively deal with life itself. We feel incapable of, and/or lack the desire to go through life on life's terms. We have low self-esteem, an inability to form solid relationships, fear-filled views of our environment, and a lack of good decision-making skills.

So we seek escape . . .

Introduction

NOBODY KNOWS FOR CERTAIN why someone is, or becomes, an addict, or why they are driven to different addictive avenues. The way I look at it, our "drug of choice", i.e., the type of addiction we fall prey to, doesn't really matter. The common denominator is that all addictions steal from us, keep us in bondage. All have the same end result: death, either in the physical sense or in the elimination of joy and freedom from our lives. Food, alcohol, work, drugs, sex, gambling, buying compulsion . . . all have one thing in common: we get addicted to them while attempting to fill a void deep within ourselves, and the lie of every addiction is that it will somehow fill this emptiness. The truth is, it never can or will. The only thing that will fill this "spiritual hole" is God-given spirituality.

Addicts Are Typically Spiritual People

Many years ago, I heard someone suggest that addicts are by nature especially spiritual people. At first, I laughed and thought, "Really, look at the mess we make of ourselves and those around us. Spiritual people? Don't think so!" However, after many years of being on a spiritual path and interacting with my fellow addicts, I completely agree with this statement.

The problem was that we pursued spirituality from the wrong source. This observation is never more obvious than as we hear newcomers to recovery express their views and insights on spiritual matters. They may have no religious background or education at all. However, when they speak of their experiences in early recovery, spirituality explodes out of their stories and reflections, even though they don't yet see or understand who the Provider of these spiritual experiences is.

As an example, a person new to recovery recently shared that, just as he was contemplating taking a drink, his sponsor called to ask him how he was doing. After the call, the thought of drinking left him and an unmistakable peace came over him. His not so surprising comment, "I'm not sure what that was all about, but I don't think this was all a coincidence."

Finding Your Higher Power

Some of us call the source of this power "spirituality". Some call it a "Higher Power". Many other names and explanations exist. I believe the power source is a loving God, whom I know through my Lord and Savior, Jesus Christ. Wherever you are in your spiritual journey, just know that you are seeking the source of the Power that can free us from the bondage of addiction ... *if we cooperate*. When you honestly and diligently seek this Power, He will guide you on the path of recovery, walk with you through the journey, and along the way, surround you with His love and strength.

The Successful Road to Recovery

It was once explained to me that when an addict hits bottom, he or she is emotionally, physically, mentally and spiritually bankrupt. When I first heard that, and even to this day, my reaction was, "Wow, that is really bad!!" Even with knowledge and acceptance of this terrible condition, learning and implementing a new set of "life tools" that are radically different than what we are accustomed to involves major surrender and willingness.

In a surrendered state and armed with willingness, the successful road to recovery is clear. We learn and practice a set of spiritually based tools that help us navigate through life. In essence, we pursue a new roadmap, a new design for living. As mentioned earlier, learning and implementing these new tools is no easy matter. Simple, but not easy. We are not used to confronting such a major challenge without engaging in our addictions. We would like to choose the much faster, simpler, immediate solutions to escape from our pain, those requiring little effort. Recovery from addiction does not work that way. If our goal is to be happy, joyous, and free, we must continually work for it. And, as I point out later in this book, the good news is that "when the student is ready, the teacher(s) will appear."

I truly believe this: a grateful, emotionally sober, spiritually-centered addict, armed with a set of practical "life tools" that he or she is willing to use on a daily basis, can turn completely away from any addiction.

There is a vast amount of information, from many sources, available on recovery. Books, television, treatment facilities, group meetings, doctors and psychologists, spiritual and religious leaders

— the list goes on and on. I have personally utilized all of these and, as a rule, found something helpful from each source.

Why this book then? What do I believe it brings to the table for addicts and those (friends and family) wanting (or desperately needing) to understand the addictive personality who is causing havoc in their lives?

The emphasis is on PRACTICALITY. In many aspects of my life, I have tended to focus on generalities, philosophies, broad-based explanations without much detail. However helpful this may be in different settings, we, as suffering addicts, desperately need specific definitions, explanations, guidelines, and instructions on how to live life in a practical way.

If there is one thing I pray you get from this book, it would be that you develop a set of simple, practical coping tools that can be applied on a daily, even minute-to-minute, basis as you journey through recovery—tools that will serve as a foundation for a new way of living, that can be used by both newcomers just entering recovery and those who have been recovering for some time. (After reading the book, my wife, who fortunately does not suffer from addiction, suggested that these tools may be helpful to anyone challenged by the trials of life and seeking a better way of living.)

Depending on where you are in recovery, some of this information may be *instructional*. However, for many of us, it will merely serve as a *reminder* of things we have already heard, understood, and incorporated in our lives, but have just forgotten momentarily.

The structure of each chapter is simple:
- Classroom Wisdom
- Tendency
- Recovery Tool
- Personal Story
- Where Do You Stand? (Questions)

Classroom Wisdom

I have included relevant quotes labeled "Classroom Wisdom." The reason for adding these came from a personal experience I had at a 12-step meeting that was held at a grammar school. As many meetings go, after the lead we broke into small groups and headed off into individual classrooms. They were decorated with colorful posters containing quotes from various sources. As the meeting proceeded, I could not help but marvel at the simplicity, wisdom, and practicality of these and other similar quotes I have found along the way. These short statements represent the essence of the tool.

Tendency

For each tool, I first explain key "Tendencies" that define us as addicts. These are things we do, think, or feel that put us in a negative state of mind or being, those scenarios that set us up for relapse and/or misery and a less than fulfilling life. We addicts all have experienced these to some degree, and I do my best to describe them in a way that you can relate to.

Recovery Tool

For each of these Tendencies, I then go on to describe a "Recovery Tool". I have learned them from many sources, and they serve both as effective antidotes to addictive behaviors as well as practical growth steps.

Personal Story

I have also included a "Personal Story" in each topic to help illustrate the experiences of recovering addicts and how they have used these tools. These stories are based on actual experiences, although they are not quoted verbatim. I use the fictional names of "Michael" and "Linda" for the purposes of anonymity.

Where Do You Stand? (Questions)

As a final consideration, included are three "Questions" that will help you assess "Where you Stand" in regards to the Tendency and Recovery Tool. To further the effectiveness of these questions, you might want to start a small group and use these topics and questions for discussion purposes, adding any new tools you discover along the way!

The order in which the topics are presented is loosely tied to my observation of the general sequence and timetable of the recovery experience. That being said, after reading and reviewing all of the tools, you may find it helpful to refer back to specific ones that become applicable to your particular situation on any given day (or minute!) as you continue on your journey of recovery.

A Special Note:

Millions of us have found a solid program of recovery through attending 12-step meetings on a regular basis, finding a sponsor, and working the 12 steps one day at a time. So it has been for me for over 22 years. In addition, I have learned that investigating and integrating any additional information and assistance, knowledge, and wisdom I can get from other sources is a real bonus. Since it is clear that physical, mental, and emotional sobriety does not come easily, why not get all the help we can?

So this book is not intended to be a substitute or replacement for the life-changing practices included in our 12-step programs. Instead, it is meant to serve as additional support and education for those suffering from addiction.

Clean, sober, and in full recovery from the power of all addictions, we can enter a new life full of hope and promise. My prayer is that this book helps you get to a place we were all meant to be: a good and peaceful place.

Let's start with a few questions right off the bat! Come back to these when you are finished reading the book.

Where Do You Stand?

Question 1: What do I hope to get out of reading and using this book?

Question 2: What can I do to ensure that I will read it completely and with an open mind?

Question 3: Will I strive to be honest, open, and willing as I consider the information presented?

Tool #1

This too shall pass
(Navigate through fears and emotional pain)

Classroom Wisdom:

"If you're going through hell, keep going." —Winston Churchill

"Pain is inevitable, suffering is optional." —Buddhist proverb

"Behind every beautiful thing, there's some kind of pain." —Bob Dylan

1. This too shall pass
(Navigate through fears and emotional pain)

Tendency:

Most addicts have an especially low tolerance for emotional pain. We have a hard time accepting feeling badly "on the inside." Others can tell us all they want that feeling this way is a natural part of life. That's good information, but we still struggle with a gnawing internal inclination that these negative feelings are not acceptable. Because of this, we constantly look for ways to escape from our feelings through destructive substance abuse, addictions, and obsessions. We got drunk, took drugs, gambled, overspent, overate, overworked, got excessively busy—anything to achieve an unhealthy, temporary "feel good/feel numb" flight from our unwanted feelings. When we escaped through our addictions, we woke to find that our troubles and negative feelings hadn't gone anywhere. Neither had our compulsive, addictive cravings . . . they most often had gotten worse.

As a normal aftermath, we dwelt in the remorse of our addictive behavior, disliked ourselves a little more, obsessed about the bleakness of our future, and moved toward isolation. As we slipped into this destructive state, we began the spiral downward. The more we needed to do positive things to get us out of this negative mind-set, *the less we were willing to do them.* The more we needed to apply our tools of recovery, *the less we called upon them.* This addictive cycle, which every addict understands, accelerated us further from the freedom that recovery brings. We eventually discovered, as a result of hitting new bottoms, that although this downward cycle is an attribute of our addictive personality, it is certainly avoidable through a change of thought and action.

Recovery Tool:

The accomplishment of working through painful feelings, emotions, and situations has a tremendously positive effect on us. It enables our growth. Working through these challenges, without using or abusing, we unquestionably come out on the other side in a different, better, and stronger place. We have matured and have taken a step that increases our confidence in our abilities to handle life—without falling back into our addictive escapism. Is it painful as we go through these times? Yes. Is hurting a necessary part of life for everyone? Yes. But avoiding working through difficult issues, and instead engaging in our addictions, results in lack of emotional growth. That's what is meant by the often discussed statement, "When I started using, I stopped growing up." Making light of this condition, I like to say, "It's hard to be an adolescent inside an adult body!"

As we go through life's challenges, we learn to accept the notion that "This too shall pass." I don't know why, but when things are difficult and painful, my present feelings tell me "this is the way it will always be. I will forever feel like I do now—awful".

When one "bad" thing happens in our lives, we tell ourselves *everything* is going wrong. This, of course, just isn't true. Life is a series of ups and downs. All situations and life stages eventually change; we mistake temporary problems for permanent ones. We need to accept the pain for now, understanding that it will be gone when it's gone. It is what it is. This acceptance diminishes depression and frustration and gives us the strength to move on, knowing there is hope for a brighter future.

We can also "act as if". While experiencing difficult situations with associated pain, we learn to "act as if" things were going smoothly. Do the next right thing. Move on to positive actions, as opposed to staying frozen and stuck in the pain, isolating and reverting to old, destructive behaviors. Practice positive "self-talk", like, "I'm coping with this problem now, not using or abusing. This is hard, but I have so many tools to help, good friends to talk with. I'm under the care of a God who will walk through this and all trials with me. I'm growing up, facing life on life's terms."

Another related tool is to monitor your actions instead of your feelings. Feelings aren't facts, actions are. We don't feel our way to good actions, we act our way to good feelings. If we wait until we *feel good* to do something positive, we may be waiting a long time. It's amazing how getting into action, doing good things for ourselves and others (even when we feel "bad"), will lift our spirits and ultimately get us to a better emotional state.

It's such a great feeling to look back and say, "Yes, I was going through an especially stressful, painful period; nonetheless, I did positive things, made progress in some areas, and grew up a little!"

One final, simple thought on this: no matter what, we "keep showing up"! We show up at our recovery groups, our family and career obligations, our service work to others, and our quiet times with God. Bring the body, and the mind and spirit will follow.

Personal Story:

Michael shared that he was early in recovery and was really struggling at work, at home, and just in general. He didn't want to drink or use, but the emotional pain was so bad he began to weep. He thought to himself, "If this is what sobriety and recovery are going to be like, I have no chance of making it."

A fellow in recovery with many years of experience recognized the pain, then quietly and with a calming spirit of kindness whispered these words, "Michael, I just want you to know that you will not feel like this forever. This too will pass. It's going to get better." These words sank deep into Michael's heart. He returned to work, made it through that day and the next, and his recovery continues through the present.

Where Do You Stand?

Question 1: How do I normally react to difficult and painful situations? What could I do to handle these situations in a better way?

Question 2: What negative messages do I need to stop telling myself, and what positive messages need to replace these?

Question 3: Do I believe that positive feelings follow positive actions? How do I know this? If I don't know this, how can I put this to use and experience this benefit?

Tool #2

No pain no gain
(Know and accept that grieving is a part of recovery)

Classroom Wisdom:

> *"One cannot get through life without pain. What we can do is choose how to use the pain life presents to us." —Bernie S. Siegel*

> *"The ultimate measure of a man is not where he stands in moments of comfort and conveniences, but where he stands at times of challenge and controversy." —Martin Luther King, Jr.*

> *"Life is 10% what happens to you, and 90% how you respond to it." —Unknown*

2. No pain no gain
(Know and accept that grieving is a part of recovery)

Tendency:

I keep thinking about the analogy of a love affair gone bad. In similar fashion, our addictions wooed us, gave us what we so desperately longed for, appeared to be the solution we had been seeking, made us feel temporarily "high". However, as in all unhealthy relationships, in the end, things fell apart. We were left in a state of despair, remorse and desperation. The only relief we could count on, albeit merely for a few minutes, was found once again in our addictions.

For an addict who is tormented by unceasing negative and obsessive thinking patterns, engaging in addictions is like taking emotional medication. We found that we needed to medicate ourselves in increasing doses to relieve the growing distress. Then, when this solution seemed like the *only* answer, our supposed "lover", our "higher power", no longer even gave us the few minutes of escape. We eventually discovered that our addiction is not a friend, lover, or higher power; it is our enemy, a lower power, a hater and destroyer of life. We finally surrendered and, with that, realized we must find a new way to live.

After "separation" from our addiction, as with all intense relationships that come to an abrupt end, grieving must take place. We feel empty, forlorn, used and abused, lied to, alone and forgotten. Something so powerful that has kept us in bondage, that snatched our minds, hearts, and souls from God, is going to eventually and predictably result in a season of pain and suffering when we leave it. That's just the way it's going to be . . . for a while.

We seek to find an explanation of why these feelings of grief are upon us, even though we are not using any longer and desire to stay that way.

Recovery Tool:

Two major elements of dealing with this harsh reality are *awareness and acceptance.*

It helps to understand that early sobriety will be painful for many reasons. This particular facet, grief, results from our radical and shocking "divorce" from our addiction. No more comfort, no more escape from life's reality. Another factor for the initial distress and remorse becomes painfully obvious: our denial is removed and we realize that during our addiction we inflicted, to varying degrees, financial, emotional, mental, and spiritual damage on ourselves and many other people who crossed our paths. It hurts badly to have flashbacks of the things we did to those who loved us.

When the fog clears, the harsh reality is that early recovery hurts, and we need to pass through this pain to experience what it means to be truly and honestly happy, joyous, and free. To get there, we must trudge through the sad, painful times and press forward until the good that lies ahead more and more becomes a reality. Believing that this joy is waiting for us in the future takes faith; the seed of this faith starts by hearing and believing in those who have been where we are and have found freedom. With their testimony as a start, we gain hope and begin doing the things that they did and do, and little by little, our lives change for the better.

Personal Story:

Linda, attending her first recovery meeting, shared her initial introduction to alcohol. She described how she felt growing up: lonely, inferior to others, indecisive, empty on the inside, etc. She told how she "met alcohol" and how all those negative feelings and attitudes about herself magically dissipated. Then, as she continued to speak, something surprising happened: a big smile came across her face and she began to clearly describe how she became obsessed with alcohol. Her demeanor and speech were very much like those of an individual who has fallen in love for the first time. This really caught everyone's attention. Then, of course, putting her head down, Linda went on to tell how her "lover-alcohol" eventually left her cold and despondent, in a worse state than ever, in every sense bound and chained like those in slavery. She explained this is what drove her to the meeting and to begin a program of recovery.

When she left, she was still hurting, but had a slight smile and a glimmer of hope for a better life.

Where Do You Stand?

Question 1: How did my addiction serve as a "higher power" in my life"? When would I turn to this "false power" for relief?

Question 2: In what ways have I experienced the pain of "divorce" from my addiction and the resulting grief from the loss?

Question 3: When, and how, did I realize my life was starting to change for the better?

Tool #3

No more me, me, me and I, I, I
(Surrender to God's will and choose His direction)

Classroom Wisdom:

> *"Make sure you are doing what God wants you to do - then do it with all your strength."* —George Washington

> *"Never be afraid to trust an unknown future to a known God."* —Corrie Ten Boom

> *"For each one of us, there is only one thing necessary: to fulfill our own destiny, according to God's will, to be what God wants us to be."* —Thomas Merton

3. No more me, me, me and I, I, I
(Surrender to God's will and choose His direction)

Tendency:

I want what I want, when I want it, and exactly the way I want it. In an angry, frustrated moment, my wife told me this was what I was like. That statement, which really rocked me, was made quite a long time ago. I won't ever forget it. It's a pretty clear picture of my general nature. It started when I was a baby, continued through my childhood, and, regretfully, is still present at times.

When I was first told about my natural tendency to always do "my will", I responded with a statement that went something like this; "*Of course* I do my own will, make my own decisions, do what I think is best for me. What else am I supposed to do?" The friend responded, "And where did that get you?" Honest answer: to a very bad place in my life — hurting, despairing, remorseful, and facing a bleak future. The follow-up statement from a mentor was, "Why don't you do someone else's will for a while and see what happens." *For a while*, the only other people I knew, trusted, and felt comfortable with in the early days of recovery were my sponsor and a few others in recovery. They routinely gave me ideas and suggestions on living, many of which were very simple, like, "Okay, so I know you feel badly today. Why don't you forget about yourself and take your kids to the playground for a while?" My typical reaction: "That doesn't make sense to me and, furthermore, *I don't want to do it.*"

Me, me, me and I, I, I —a common and simple underlying current of what drives us —selfishness and self-centeredness.

Stubbornly following our distorted wills, especially when in the throes of addiction, is a form of insanity. When we acted alone, on our own strength and understanding, there was little thought of a higher purpose in our life or in the world around us. Our misguided wills, fueled by our growing addictions, drove our compulsive attempts to make our world conform to the way we thought it should be. Self-gratification, immediate pleasure, and lack of concern for others were evident in many of our decisions and actions.

Moreover, once we stop using and/or abusing, it doesn't mean that our self-centered, pleasure-seeking personalities promptly change. We are reluctant to do things that take time, that are difficult, that cause us to stretch, that appear boring, that require pushing the boundaries of courage and faith, that require humility—in other words, things that don't bring us immediate gratification and those that come at a cost to our comfort, security, or inflated ego. The thought and actual act of doing something, simply because we believe it is God's will for us, involves an attitude change of a large scale. Some people have labeled this change a "spiritual awakening": an awakening that involves a radically different perception of ourselves and others, in our desires and attitudes, in our intentions and actions, in our beliefs and convictions—in other words, in the core of who we are.

Recovery Tool:

Thy will, not mine, be done.

I like the definition of "my will" as one's combined *thoughts* and *actions*. Given a new spiritual insight, I once shared at a meeting, "When my will is aligned with God's will, I'm in a very good place. It's only when our wills differ that conflict and struggle take place." This rather simple thought implies that I have an understanding of the difference between my will and God's. I can honestly say that very often I am given this understanding. I'm confident that as we pursue our spiritual paths of recovery, we will learn, with an increasing degree of confidence, God's will for us. Tools to help us discern God's will abound. Here are a few that help me: spiritual friends and mentors, the Bible, recovery books, church, spiritual retreats, spiritual books, talks and sermons on God's will, and the concepts presented in the 12 steps of recovery.

I have learned to seek, and, through prayer and meditation, many times hear God's will for me in His "small, still voice". He whispers promptings such as, "Rick, don't do that, it's not good for you; you should call this person; why don't you stop fretting and go to a meeting; tell your wife you're sorry," etc. I continue to grow in my ability to sense when God "speaks to me" in this way.

Likewise, I have other thoughts that come into my head that I can tell you with certainty are not those of God! Discernment between these sources gets easier as time goes on. It's important that we check in with spiritual advisers and mentors on what we're "hearing", especially at major decision points in our lives. With our natural, strong-willed tendency to do what we want, it's easy to rationalize wrong behavior and choices as "God directed".

It is common to hear in the recovery community discussions regarding God's will based on this premise: "I'm not always sure what the will of God *is*, but I almost always know what His will *isn't!*" Clear examples of not doing His will would be: harming others, being dishonest, or falling back into our addictions. One powerful, simple tool that is described with a bit of humor is the *awareness* of when you are about to do something and **your stomach begins hurting—don't do it!** Our spirit may well be informing us that we are about to do something wrong, something not good for us. Many people have suggested that we were born with this "instinct" or "God conscience". Another explanation relates to our childhoods: "Remember when you were little and you were about to steal something and you *just knew* this was wrong"?

Okay. So let's say we are confident that we have concluded what the will of God is in a particular situation. Great, problem solved. Simple, right? Not that easy. Just knowing the will of God, of course, is a long distance from *doing* the will of God. I like the saying, "You can't *think your way* into a new way of *living* . . . you have to *live your way* into a new way of thinking!" Recently I imagined this metaphor that painted a picture of the gap between understanding and doing God's will. It's as if we are standing on a cliff holding onto the knowledge of what God's will is for us; however, to receive the promises that come with doing what is right, we must cross over a valley to a mountain on the other side. The only way to do this is to build a bridge named "willingness". And one thing is for certain, *only you, with the help of God, can build that bridge. No other human being can build it for you.*

Sometimes it's just plain hard to do the right thing, especially when it takes something from us that we enjoy or desire or that brings us comfort. Doing God's will may require sacrifice or temporary discomfort. Over time, we learn to call upon a strength not our own to give us the power to follow through on what we discern is God's will. We find that this Power, coming from outside ourselves, is the only way we can gain the willingness to do what we must to attain the incredible peace resulting from *living* God's will in our lives.

I have found the following to be true, in countless number of personal incidents regarding this subject: when I'm confident of what God's will for me is in a particular situation, and I consciously decide *not to do it*, it *never* ends satisfactorily, either in terms of the actual consequences or, equally important, in how it settles within my spirit.

When, on the other hand, I believe I know what God's will is for me *and I do it*, it *always* turns out for my good, either in the outcomes themselves or in the wonderful feeling I have in my spirit as a result of trying to do God's will. Not surprisingly, this axiom is especially true when there is a wide gap between what *I want to do* and what I believe *God wants me to do.*

Personal Story:

After several months in a 12-step recovery program, Michael was asked to speak (tell his story) at a very large, "open speaker" meeting on a Saturday night. Somewhere close to 100 recovering addicts and their families would be present. Michael's initial reaction to the request was quick, simple, and full of fear: "I cannot speak in front of this group. I'm not ready for this. I won't be able to do it." The requestor just smiled and said, "Oh, yes, you can. Just ask God for help and show up. It will be fine." Michael just stood and stared as his "friend" walked away.

In the days leading up to the Saturday meeting, Michael's anxiety, fear, and projections were overwhelming. He thought, "This can't be the will of God. I wouldn't feel like this if it were. I'm not sure I am going to be able to do this, with or without God's help. "

Hours before the 8 p.m. meeting started, all Michael could think of doing was to go to the chapel in the hospital where the meeting was held. He had a very honest, direct. and one-way talk with God. His comments went something like this: "Okay, Lord, I am going to ask you to help me with this. Because if my will prevails, my 'talk' will go like this: my name is Michael and I'm an alcoholic. Thank you and good night!" That wouldn't be a very beneficial evening for the people who traveled from all over to hear a talk about the pain of addiction and the hope of recovery, would it, he thought? As time neared for him to go to the podium to speak, almost as a last, desperate cry to God, Michael made this final request, "If this is truly Your will, I only ask that something I say tonight helps just one person in the room."

Michael spoke from the heart. He told his story of addiction and recovery for the full 45 minutes. He paused at times, not quite sure how the words were actually coming out. It was if he were outside himself looking in and listening to the words that were being spoken. After his talk, the floor was opened for comments, as was done in each speaker meeting. One fellow, Eric, raised his hand, stood, and slowly said these words: "Michael, I don't know if you helped anyone else in this room tonight, but I want you to know you helped me. Thank you." Michael sat somewhat stunned as he instantly remembered his last request of God in the chapel.

Many years later, he thought about the events of that night and his slow, but continual progress in accepting these words: "Your will, not mine, be done."

Where Do You Stand?

Question 1: Am I committed to *trying* to discern and do God's will *always?* If not, what hinders me from this, and why?

Question 2: Can I recall a situation where I was clearly not doing God's will and one where I clearly was? What were the results of each? What were my feelings toward each?

Question 3: What is God's will for me right now?

Tool #4

When all else fails
(Do the next right thing)

Classroom Wisdom:

"Those who try to do something and fail are infinitely better than those who try to do nothing and succeed." —Lloyd Jones

"The secret of getting ahead is getting started. The secret of getting started is breaking your complex overwhelming tasks into small manageable tasks, and then starting on the first one." —Mark Twain

"It's the action, not the fruit of the action, that's important. You have to do the right thing. It may not be in your power, may not be in your time, that there will be any fruit. But that doesn't mean you stop doing the right thing. You may never know what results come from your action. But if you do nothing, there will be no result." —Mahatma Gandhi

4. When all else fails
(Do the next right thing)

Tendency:

As addicts, our minds typically generate negative thinking as the default. We can take the smallest obstacle, challenge, or problem and parlay it into a scenario of doom and gloom without any basis in fact. A small decline in our financial situation can take our imagination all the way to financial ruin. A disagreement with our boss can lead us to thinking we will be fired at any moment. A resentment against our spouse can have us separated forever and never speaking again . . . and so on. When we allow this negative thinking spiral to happen, without taking necessary measures to stop the "disaster in our minds", we sit frozen in a state of fear and bewilderment, typically accompanied by inaction, isolation, and paranoia. We are frightened. We hate the way we feel, so we fall to our addiction, and our mental condition worsens.

In contemplating disastrous scenarios, we then imagine solutions to these problems that are equally unrealistic. We dream of major positive changes in our life situations without considering or accepting the tangible efforts required to achieve such changes. Maybe we will win the lottery and our financial situation will be resolved. Maybe we will move to a new city where life will be better. Surely the upcoming vacation we are taking will pull the family together and get us back on track. Or, that other person we really like will be the perfect companion and we will be happy once again.

In this state of mind, we do not think clearly or rationally. Our inflated egos, along with our inferiority complexes, combine to generate totally unrealistic pictures of the future.

Recovery Tool:

One tool that has helped me tremendously with this debilitating problem is simply *doing the next right thing*. Now implementing this antidote to fear, isolation, and inaction can mean many different things and be applied at many levels. The easiest way to describe this tool would be taking *the next small action* that moves us toward the positive and away from isolation, fear, and immobility. Just getting into action, regardless of how minor, is the key to moving forward. For example, if our experience tells us that going to a 12-step meeting will get us out of our funk, then it may well be that asking our Higher Power for help getting up off the couch, finding our car keys, and then going to the car are the small but critical "next right steps" needed to get us moving in the right direction. Likewise, letting our sponsor or friend know what is going on with us may require the willingness to take just a small step, like picking up the phone and dialing the number.

Instead of dwelling on how an entire series of actions is too overwhelming given the mind-set we are in, the helpful course is to just identify and put into action *only the next simple steps* to get us moving on a positive path. When we do the required steps, one by one, asking for help and thanking Him along the way, it is amazing how the fog can lift. In turn, feelings of despair and depression change to those of progress and hope. As we are taking these needed actions, if the thoughts of doom and gloom continue, like an unwanted chorus of clamoring negativity, we can say this simple prayer (as many times as needed): "God, please don't let me think this way." It's amazing how powerful a simple prayer like this can help us think, live, and act better.

Why not start our right actions for the day before we even get out of bed in the morning? Maybe a prayer like, "I love you, Lord, and I need your help today. Help me keep my thoughts on You, Lord. Amen."

Personal Story:

Michael was early in recovery, and depression, anxiety, and insomnia dogged him day after day. He had been told that his nervous system was only starting to return to normal, so he should expect to feel out of whack, anxious, and stressed for some time to come.

On this particular morning, Michael woke up after having several vivid nightmares about relapsing. He could only lay motionless for some time and finally was able to conclude that these were only dreams. His physical reaction told him they were as close to reality as you can get.

His thoughts eventually turned to his mother who was in the hospital, dying from cancer and not having much longer to live. He had visited her during his days of drinking, but was there only in body. During these difficult preceding years of his mother's decline, he had assumed the only way he could physically visit her was in a numbed state.

Frozen in fear and anxiety he thought, "No way I can go to see her today. I'm just not capable of doing this. I'll probably not be able to go in. Or, if I see her, I'll break down and make her feel worse than she already feels. I just can't do this. I can't even get out of bed."

Then the guidance he had heard from his "professors" in the 12-step recovery program came to him in a clear, distinct way. Waves of ideas he had heard floated in like, "Ask God for help, then get into action." "Do just the smallest, next best thing you should do, and then thank God for his help." "He can, you can't, let Him. Let's not spend energy on cleaning up the wreckage of the future!"

Armed with these ideas, and a new glimmer of hope, Michael thought, "Well I could get out of bed and take a shower." He asked God for help and showered. "Thank you, God." He went on to get dressed, asking God for help and then thanking Him. Then to the car, keys into the ignition, navigating the drive to the hospital. All along the way, "Please help. Thanks." Finally, through the hospital door, up the elevator and into the hospital room. Again, "Please help. Thanks." In a strange sense, like waking up from a dream, he realized that he was now standing in front of his mom, smiling, putting the simple cross on her that she had asked for. Unlike his nightmarish thoughts just earlier in the morning, Michael now was experiencing the comforting realization that God had helped him do what he could never have done by himself.

When Michael finally lay in bed that night, he reflected on the day with amazement. "How did I do this?" he pondered. The answer came at once: "You asked for help and you got it. Doing just one next right thing at a time."

He thanked God for His help and fell peacefully asleep.

Where Do You Stand?

Question 1: In what ways do I tend to think negatively? Describe and give examples.

Question 2: When have I been stuck in a place seemingly unable to move forward? What did I do? Explain.

Question 3: When did I try doing a series of "next right things" to come out of a slump or funk? What was the outcome? What is the next right thing for me to do **right now**?

Tool #5

Turn the "m" in me upside down
(Get into fellowship/ Don't isolate)

Classroom Wisdom:

"Loneliness leads to nothing good, only detachment. And sometimes the people who most need to reach out are the people least capable of it." —Joss Whedon

"Solitude is fine but you need someone to tell that solitude is fine." —Honoré de Balzac

*"The **I** in illness is isolation, and the crucial letters in wellness are **we**." —Unknown*

5. Turn the "m" in me upside down
(Get into fellowship/ Don't isolate)

Tendency:

When things get difficult and life throws us curve balls, we like escape, to go to our "caves" and hide out. This could be a physical place or just a lonely dwelling spot within our hearts. Hiding there, we accept no visitors, take no phone calls, and avoid any intimate, interpersonal communications with others. We just isolate, obsess on what is troubling us, and fight our addictive impulses. We sometimes try to convince ourselves that we alone can think through the solution that will lift us out of this dark place.

Or we may decide that feeling this way is more familiar and comfortable than seeking help. We may try to distract ourselves with some meaningless activities, e.g., television, video games, surfing the net, etc., so we don't have to deal with those recurring negative feelings that trigger our compulsions. By being alone in our own heads, rehashing the same dismal thoughts, avoiding positive actions to address the problems, we feed our negativity, allowing it to take us to ever-worsening levels of depression, anger and inaction.

This addictive, negative state invites us to *isolate, to keep us alone, disconnected from people and God.* For people who suffer from depression (many or even most of us), this is a particularly prevalent and destructive tendency. As an extreme outcome, I can't count the number of times I have heard about addicts dying *alone*, almost always in some lonely, dark place. I'll say it again: they end up desolate, disconnected from the fellowship, from friends and family, and trying to hide from God. **In other words, unwilling, and therefore, unable to connect with the <u>solution</u>.**

Recovery Tool:

We connect ourselves with friends, family and the fellowship, *especially when that is the last thing we want to do.* Talking to others, especially those in recovery, and sharing what is going on in our heads and with our emotions has a healing, relieving effect on us. Just being around others in recovery, going to a meeting, stopping for coffee afterward, being part of general life discussions, etc., can go a long way to changing our negative state of mind to a positive one. It works, even if we can only contribute a little, or even nothing, to the conversation. God wants us to be around other souls. Life was meant to be lived in community. Connecting with others is a powerful, spiritual antidote to the negative powers that drive us to an inner world of despair and loneliness. Although recovery is an "inside job", it blossoms with the support, companionship, and love of others.

We make fellowship automatic. We schedule someone to pick us up once a week for a meeting. We can join a fellowship club, e.g., a golf league, book club, etc. We commit to going to celebrations, picnics, parties, and other social functions, including weddings and funerals. We schedule regular times to meet with our sponsors and mentors for dinner or maybe coffee and a piece of pie. If we are uncomfortable when we start engaging in these activities, we remember that good feelings will eventually follow good actions.

It is also important that we build and nurture long-term, deep relationships with others. This is not an easy thing to do for people who tend to isolate. It takes willingness, effort, discipline, and commitment. We can start with just one or two individuals, selected on the basis of trust and an instinctive feel that we can relate to them and are comfortable in their presence.

Then the real work begins. We put ourselves out by calling them and suggesting times to meet, e.g., have coffee, go to events, have dinner, etc. We begin opening ourselves up so that these people can get to know who we really are. We can start with small talk, the topic doesn't really matter. Then, when the time is right, we ease into our personal selves. They eventually hear all about us, good and bad. When we release the burdens we have in the company of these friends, we walk away, lighter in spirit, with a more realistic perspective on our situation, usually with helpful suggestions, and feeling like we are part of the human race.

The challenge is that relationships take time to build, involve risk, and have ups and downs, good times and bad. We might get angry, disappointed, have hurt feelings, etc., that we need to overcome as we keep moving forward in these relationships. Like all of life, making friends and keeping them for long periods is not easy, does not happen perfectly, involves risk, and takes effort and commitment on our part. In addition to these close relationships with a few, we remember that just being around people, especially those in recovery, has a healing, positive effect on our spirits.

We come to understand that addiction rages in the "I", recovery is fueled by the "We". In summary, we learn to turn the "m" in me upside down.

Personal Story:

Disgusted with the way his life was headed, Michael decided that he had to figure out why he was so messed up. Why did he feel lost? All alone in the world? Without a lot of hope? No peace of mind, ever? He concluded that, with his intelligence and ability to solve problems, he would be able to successfully analyze this problem, come to an answer, and develop a plan of action—all by himself.

So he bought a bottle of vodka, went down to his basement, told his family not to bother him, took the phone off the hook, and began to think. He drank the bottle of vodka to "clear his head and relax". People called to see how he was doing, since they knew he was troubled as a result of his drinking. Michael didn't want to talk. His family nervously waited for him to emerge from the basement, hopeful that somehow he would be better. Michael stayed in the basement. Treatment centers waited, doctors were available for assistance. Michael kept drinking. Somewhere a sponsor was ready to help. A strong fellowship of recovering alcoholics was active and close by, ready to encourage and help all newcomers.

But Michael didn't think he needed any of them. As he drifted into a state of drunkenness, he concluded that he was now just too tired to think any more. Tomorrow he would work harder to find the answer—all by himself.

Soon afterward, Michael hit bottom and now is in recovery. He understands that addiction was his problem, and he focuses his time working on the solution. He limits his time alone and instead spends many healthy and fulfilling hours with his family, friends, and participating in recovery fellowship.

Where Do You Stand?

Question 1: When have I ever found myself isolating from people and life? What causes me to do this? How do I feel when I do this?

Question 2: When I isolate, what "caves" do I hide in?

Question 3: What types of fellowship activities are most appealing to me? What would it take for me to engage in these activities when what I really want to do is isolate?

Tool #6

Listen up now
(Learn to listen, not just hear)

Classroom Wisdom:

"There are people who, instead of listening to what is being said to them, are already listening to what they are going to say themselves." —Albert Guinon

"To say that a person feels listened to means a lot more than just their ideas get heard. It's a sign of respect. It makes people feel valued." —Deborah Tannen

"So when you are listening to somebody, completely, attentively, then you are listening not only to the words, but also to the feeling of what is being conveyed, to the whole of it, not part of it." —Jiddu Krishnamurti

6. Listen up now
(Learn to listen, not just hear)

Tendency:

For some reason, it's hard for us to listen. A better description is that, although we may hear, we are not good at listening. Most of the time we are so "into our heads" with our internal chatterbox chirping away, it is impossible to listen to anyone else, including God. Further, once we decide we are going to respond to the bits and pieces we have heard, formulating our response then dominates our minds, and additional listening is not possible. Our inability to sit still and calmly focus on what others are saying is difficult, especially in the early stages of withdrawal from addiction. Let's face it: our nervous systems are under siege and our mental and emotional faculties are functioning less than normally. We are generally nervous, fearful, and projecting all sorts of negativity. In this heightened state of dis-ease (pun intended), active listening is just likely not going to happen.

Not being able to focus on what others are saying is a hindrance to our growth, since we need the input and insights of others to help change our thinking. In our addiction, we were alone in our minds most of the time, whether or not we were around people. As selfishness and self-centeredness gain a growing stranglehold in our lives, the guiding and wise voices and thoughts of others, including God, become increasingly distant and faint.

Recovery Tool:

The major tool here is practice and patience. We eventually learn to "listen hard" to what others are saying and learn to ignore the "committee of voices" convening in our heads when others are speaking.

When we begin to truly absorb what others say, we are able to consider the significance of what has been said. Our spirits capture the words, and later, sometimes much later, they will come back to us in a way that we truly understand them. This input becomes a source of needed insight and serves as a basis for changes we need to make in our way of thinking and living.

On a practical level, it definitely helps to focus in on the individual who is speaking, making eye contact and giving nonverbal acknowledgement that we are listening to what the person is saying. A related and equally important skill to practice is ignoring distractions, e.g., noises and other forms of disturbances that impede our ability to concentrate on the person speaking. If obsessive thoughts invade our minds, we can repeat, "God, don't let me think like this" or "God, please take this thought away." Then we double our efforts to focus and listen well.

As a side benefit to active listening, it's amazing how much others appreciate it when they know we are paying attention to them. Once we realize this, it encourages us to keep up with the practice. We also notice that when we attentively listen to others, many times this courtesy is returned to us. It's reassuring to know that at least one person is paying attention to what we have to say.

We also learn to listen to the still, small voice of God, which plays an important part in our journey of recovery. Some people describe this inner thought as instinct, intuition, conscience, or insight. Label it as you may, I have come to believe it is God helping us. Although it has taken time for me to learn how to discern His voice, a skill that has been enhanced by prayer and meditation, once I "got it", this recognition serves as a calming and distinct source of understanding of His will for me. One thing that has helped me with recognizing His voice is how it always comes in a clear, caring, and kind manner. Always.

This important change in our communication skills corresponds with our growth in recovery, since it signifies a focus away from ourselves, and a positive movement toward concern, attention, and respect for others.

Personal Story:

Linda was new to recovery and to the tables at meetings where members discussed their recovery journeys. As the first person started sharing, Linda thought about how much trouble she was in, how her life had become a train wreck. When the next person began speaking, Linda wondered if she should be spending her time at this meeting or be looking for a job. When the next person spoke, Linda became distracted by the noise in the cafeteria and the workers nearby who were loud and annoying. Linda started to wonder how long this meeting was going to last, since she had a lot of important tasks to complete that day. When it was her turn to speak, Linda passed, since she hadn't heard a word that had been said and really didn't have a clue as to what the topic was.

Since then, Linda has learned that it's very important to focus on what each person is saying, for a couple of reasons. First, through many personal experiences, it has become crystal clear to her that God speaks through others, and many times she gets the answer she needs from what they say. (At one point she got so much specific help from those at her table, she wondered if they'd had a pre-meeting to discuss her problem!) Second, Linda figured out that she sure liked it when people paid attention to what she was saying, and she wants to do the same for them. She smiles at the thought of her full participation.

Where Do You Stand?

Question 1: What kind of a listener do I think I am? Decide, and then ask three people who know you what kind of a listener you are.

Question 2: Where, and in what ways, could I practice becoming a better listener?

Question 3: When have I heard the "small, still voice of God"? Describe.

Tool #7

S.O.S
(Ask for help)

Classroom Wisdom:

"It's not the load that breaks you down; it's the way you carry it."
—Lena Horne

"Give all your worries and cares to God, for He cares about you."
—Peter 5:7 (New Living Translation)

"Keep in mind that part of growing up is learning how to deal with difficult issues, and the benefits can be great if you have the courage to ask for help. Human beings are not designed to go through life alone. No one has to bear the burden of the tough times all by themselves." —Jack Canfield, Mark Victor Hansen, and Kimberly Kirberger

7. S.O.S
(Ask for help)

Tendency:

Many of us grow up with the idea that we must learn to do things by and for ourselves. We have to stand on our own two feet, always. So we learn not to seek help from anyone; we certainly don't want to *depend* on someone to provide us with the important or even critical assistance we need. When things get difficult and problems arise, we tend to get even more "independent", not sharing what's happening with others and stubbornly not asking for help. It may unnecessarily take days, weeks, or even years to get resolution to problems or situations we encounter as a result of our obstinate and foolish "John Wayne" (I can handle everything myself)-like attitude. "So what," we say. "We are used to living like this. It's comfortable. Our problems are our problems. We will deal with them miserably and ineffectively and feel as frustrated as we want to while going through it." Great example of "stinkin' thinkin'", isn't it?

Unfortunately, when others come in contact with us, they will also feel the effects of our unpleasant state. After damage is inevitably inflicted on these innocent bystanders, we say, "So what? That's their problem. They shouldn't have gotten in our way." Then, to make matters worse, we isolate in a hopeless attempt to "figure things out" by ourselves, even though in the past our best thinking got us nowhere except to a worsened mental and emotional condition.

Asking for help requires a humble attitude. Our pride and ego erect a strong blockade to reaching out for support. When considering asking for help, we may nix the idea by saying things to ourselves like: "They don't have time; they don't really care; I'm just bothering them; why would they do this for me?" With these thoughts rolling through our heads, it just gets more difficult to reach out for assistance. We have a hard time accepting that if the people are not able, or don't want to help, they will just tell us so; if they are able and willing to help, they will do so, ungrudgingly, as we would for them.

Recovery Tool:

Ask for help. There is nothing shameful or demeaning in getting assistance when we need it. Not asking is willful and egocentric. Reaching out demonstrates and builds an attitude of humility by inviting others into our lives. This type of humility can help us grow emotionally as well as just simply providing us with the practical assistance we need to get something done. "Help" can take many, many forms: running a problem or difficult situation by someone looking for their input, asking for a ride when we can't drive, or having a cup of coffee with someone to unload a worry or problem.

Whom should we ask? I would strongly suggest we start with . . . God(!), immediately upon recognition of a need. I love the suggestion of not complicating the request. Just plain, "Help!", like a child would call out to a parent, "Dad, Mom, help, please." After asking God for help, we then call or visit our trusted advisors, our mentors and coaches, people whom we trust, whose lives are a reflection of their core beliefs. These are people whose beliefs and values are fundamentally aligned with ours, people we respect. Many times asking for help involves our family. Letting them know that we need their help, opening ourselves up in terms of our needs, can bring our most personal relationships to a new level of intimacy.

And let us not forget the other side of the coin. The people we engage most times consider our request an honor and, as it turns out, provides *them* with an opportunity to experience the gift of giving as well. You will hear this gratitude often and with great sincerity, when the "helper" thanks us for reaching out to them for support.

One caution on the topic of asking for help is the situation where a person becomes overly dependent on others to take on his or her problems. We need to accept and own the fact that although most people are willing to help us, we are ultimately responsible for our own well-being.

Personal Story:

Michael was early in recovery and knew he needed to get to a lot of meetings to stay clean and sober. Not having a driver's license any longer represented a problem, since it was many miles to the nearest meeting. But he walked every day as much from will power as the growing understanding of the dedication and discipline it takes to embrace recovery. As people at the meetings became aware that Michael had no transportation, they began offering rides. Michael's response was always a polite, "Thanks, but I'm doing okay." One day in the dead of winter, Michael headed off to the meeting and a blinding snowstorm started. It was too late for him to head back home, and he wouldn't anyway due to his strong self-will. He stopped for a cup of coffee and wondered why he just wouldn't accept offers of rides. He began to question his attitude and, contemplating the brutal walk, a spark of willingness came over him.

As he started walking again toward the meeting, a car pulled up and asked him if he needed a ride. He had never seen this person before, but he immediately said, "Yes, I do." As he sat in the passenger seat, he noticed a little black book on the person's dashboard and recognized it immediately. It was a "24-hour meditation book" used in many programs of recovery. Michael smiled and asked the person about the book. "Oh, yes," the person responded, "I've been in the program for some time."

Michael asked, "So did you recognize me when you pulled up in your car?"

"No," the driver responded, "something just told me to stop to ask you if you needed a ride."

Michael immediately made the spiritual connection between his spark of willingness and God's response. He went on to get many rides to and from meetings and now does the same for others, since his license has been reinstated.

Where Do You Stand?

Question 1: Do I generally find it difficult to ask for help? If so, why?

Question 2: Under what conditions do I find it most difficult to ask for help? Why?

Question 3: What are some examples of where I should have asked for help and didn't? Where I did? Whom did I ask, and why them?

Tool #8

It is what it is
(Live life on life's terms)

Classroom Wisdom:

"Do not push the river; it will flow by itself." —*Chinese proverb*

"I'm not afraid of storms, for I'm learning to sail my ship."
—*Louisa May Alcott*

*"Your living is determined not so much by what life brings to
you as by the attitude you bring to life; not so much by what
happens to you as by the way your mind looks at what happens."*
—*Khalil Gibran*

8. It is what it is
(Live life on life's terms)

Tendency:

When things in life do not go "our way", we typically blame other people, places, and things for the negative state of mind that follows. Then we are tempted to escape from the situations we perceive we cannot control. Instead of examining the problem for what it is, finding the appropriate solution and implementing it, we find it much easier to numb ourselves. Or, in a supposedly "improved approach", we don't engage in our addiction, but miserably trudge thru the difficult times restless, irritable, and discontented, making our lives and those around us unpleasant, cold, and cheerless.

We suffer from a lack of coping skills that we should have learned and developed during our years of active addiction. At times, we don't like how fast things are going, at other times, how long they take. We do not effectively or appropriately deal with work challenges, relationship disputes, financial setbacks, or even positive events like promotions and celebrations. Again, it is clear that we failed to acquire an effective set of tools that could guide us, with some level of sanity and maturity, through the peaks and valleys that life brings.

To justify this inability to cope, we consciously or subconsciously think thoughts like, "This isn't fair. This should not be happening to me. Why did this happen now? God hates me. I'm being punished. One more problem. Another bad thing in my life, why can't I get a break? How long will this bad luck go on? I'm trying to do the right thing, why don't they see this? I just need a little relief."

When we have success we think, "You bet I'm going to celebrate. I deserve this. I did it all by myself. See, my life is good, and my addiction only adds to the pleasure of it all." Or, in the midst of our successes, we may have forebodings of how our good fortune will be taken from us at any moment.

We want to know with certainty what the future will bring. We want to lock it down and be assured that things will happen the way we think they should, since we are, of course, running the show. Trying to control every little thing in our life, to our way of liking, exhausts us. It can't work, regardless of how hard we try. Over control saps our energy and frustrates us to the point where it's really difficult to be useful to ourselves and others. This frustrated state can lead to addictive behaviors, with the ensuing, vicious cycle of remorse and despair, and the downward cycle continues.

I have a background in project management. I know how to create detailed project plans that depict the step-by-step actions necessary to complete a project. When they do, I am one happy camper. When they don't, it's not good to be around me. Things in life never will go according to plan, especially plans we develop in an addiction-driven state of mind. I often hear, "If you want to get God to laugh, tell him *your* plans."

Recovery Tool:

We develop a set of coping tools that allow us to effectively deal with life, both the good and bad. We build an arsenal of healthy and mature spiritual practices. These are tools and practices like calling our sponsor, friends, and mentors when we are obsessing over something; going to a recovery meeting and engaging in the discussion as best we can; engaging in physical exercise; helping others; acknowledging the things we have to be grateful for; asking for input from others when we don't know the answer. Most importantly, we don't run away and hide, using addiction to escape from reality. We do the best we can and learn the lessons we need to learn.

We learn to *wear life like a loose garment.* We go with the flow that life brings us, as best we can. It's fine to have plans, but when things don't work out as we would have them, we need to **adjust.** We let go of our strong desire to *control* people, places and things, to grab them by the throat and not let go. If we constantly fight the things in life that come along that we don't like, we are never going to be "happy, joyous, and free". We determine if and where we need to change direction, beginning with our thinking. Maybe it's a slight change, maybe a major shift. Then we make the adjustment with as little resentment and resistance as possible.

If circumstances are the primary basis for our happiness, we will not achieve any consistent level of serenity. The more we can accept things as they are, instead of how we want them to be, the better life will become for us. When things need changing for the right reasons, we change them. We learn it is okay to take care of ourselves.

Another good tool: *Live in the here and now.* Not easy for us to do. What I have learned is that things in our lives *always* change. Life is cyclical. We go through smooth and difficult times on a continuing basis. Our circumstances and moods go up and down, no matter how we try to control and manage things around us. So the attitude I have found for this life cycle is two-fold: first, when things are smooth and going well, just enjoy it! It's not going to last forever but so what? Let's just go for the ride, savoring the blessings that have fallen upon us, and accept these times for what they are. We thank God for these smooth and serene seasons.

Second, when we run into tough patches, we make whatever changes we can and then realize and accept the rest as the way it is *for now.* Yes, it's difficult. Yes, we don't like it, but it's not always going to be like this. We try to remember that even though the storm rages, we have been through other storms before. They don't last, and we came through them just fine. We thank God for these periods of challenge and growth.

We can have hope for a brighter time; we don't force things, ultimately making the situation worse by trying to prematurely end the difficult period, when we just need to ride it out. We accept that for now things are tough, not going the way we would like. In these times, we learn it's best to just do the next right thing. A good analogy: life is like running a race. Sometimes we get stuck in the mud; each step is like drudgery. We make very little progress, but even so, *we are moving forward.* And then, at other times, we are running forward at full speed. Nothing gets in our way. We are light and breezy . . .

Personal Story:

Linda was diagnosed with cancer many years ago. Surgery had been successful, and each year afterword she would get an annual checkup to make sure she remained cancer free. She received a clean bill of health for many years in a row . . . until this year. She received a frightening call from the hospital. They told her they saw something in the test results that did not look good. They asked her to come to the doctor's office next week for further tests.

Linda's obvious immediate reaction was concern and fear. After the shock of the news, she remembered that she had made a dinner date for that night with her daughter to celebrate her birthday. Her first thought was, "Well, I certainly can't do that now. I am too upset. I'll just call and cancel."

Then a new insight hit her. Why should she cancel? Why should she miss the happiness and joy of celebrating her daughter's birthday? She would not only go to dinner but also fully enjoy her daughter's company and catch up on all that was happening in her life. She realized she had no control over what was going to happen next week and . . . she was not going to let this news take away her inner joy and freedom and those of her daughter. She concluded, "It is what it is. I will turn the results over to God and enjoy the next week of my life."

Linda went to dinner with her daughter as planned and had a joyful time. The following week the results of further tests came out. There were no signs of cancer; her health was excellent. Linda reflected, "Thanks God, a whole week of good living not lost to fear and worry about what Your future plans held for me."

Where Do You Stand?

Question 1: How am I currently doing in the area of living life on life's terms?

Question 2: What things am I holding on to, or running away from, that are hurting me? Am I willing to change?

Question 3: When have I been stuck in the mud? What tools did I use to get out and begin running again?

Tool #9

Huddle up
(Get mentors)

Classroom Wisdom:

"Lost is the man who chooses foolish companions, but good company paves the straight road of wisdom." —Azusa Pacific University Student

"Everyone hears what you say. Friends listen to what you say. Best friends listen to what you don't say." —Unknown

"When it hurts to look back, and you're afraid to look ahead, you can look beside you and your best friend will be there." —Unknown

9. Huddle up
(Get mentors)

Tendency:

Our independent attitude is tied in with our nature of wanting to do things one way, our way, the only way. We like to make decisions on our own. We are honestly not interested in what others (even those who care deeply about us) think about our situation or what advice they may have to improve our views or direction. Why should we share our situation, outline our plan of action, and then be told that this is probably not the way to go? Who wants to hear that? Aren't we the masters of our own destiny? Don't we know ourselves and our situation better than anyone else? Aren't we really good at making decisions on our own?

That's really a curious attitude on our part, since most, if not all, of the trouble we got into was based solely on our own best thinking. We miss the fact that we are seeing things through a very narrow, sometimes distorted lens, a perspective based only on our limited experience and sometimes our misguided or flawed attitudes and beliefs. I experienced this phenomenon early in recovery when, after one year of sobriety, I did a self-analysis of how many meetings I should attend per week. When I ran *my* decision by a fellow recovering person with long-term sobriety, he asked, "Why would you make this decision on your own? Just curious, wasn't it your best thinking that got you locked up in the treatment center?" That hurt. However, he was right! It was the truth. Truth received sheds a bright light on our misdirected thinking.

I have seen people who take this solo attitude and make disastrous decisions, only to say afterward that it was only someone or something outside their control that caused their plans to fail. You would think that when this approach of stubborn independence failed, we would surrender and start asking for other opinions, suggestions, insights, or advice. Right? Not so in many cases. Many times we just default to the same lone approach, again and again, suffering the same results. For some reason, we don't believe that people who care about us, some with years of recovery and strong spiritual connections, have anything to offer that would help our not-so-unique situation. Or is it that we really don't want to listen, and then act upon ideas that will have us do things we don't want to do or stop doing things we're doing?

Recovery Tool:

We develop a small group of close advisors, confidants, mentors, or whatever else you want to call these chosen few. They are the comrades who get to know us better than anyone else, in many cases better than our own family members. Over time, they get to know who we really are on the inside, what our strengths and weaknesses are, what defects cause us problems, what our past has been like, and the plans we have for the future. These are people we can call or talk with who don't require a lengthy background before we explain our current question, problem, or joy. Over time, we get comfortable exposing our fears and weaknesses to them, since we trust their confidence and lose our fear of being judged by them.

We ask God to help us identify who our mentors should be. We listen to what they have to say, and watch how they live their lives, evaluating them against the old question: "Are they walking the walk, or just talking the talk?" We have a comfort when we are around them and look forward to seeing them in our fellowship circles. The best ones are good listeners and those who have traveled down similar paths as ours. I believe another important criterion is that they have compatible spiritual beliefs, as for many, this serves as a cornerstone to the way we approach life in general. Finally, it's important that they be courageous and caring enough to hold us accountable; that means telling us things we need to hear but truly don't want to be told. This quality in others is hard to find.

We run our ideas and plans by these people, and the larger the decision, the more important to do so. We have an attitude of openness and willingness; we listen and consider their counsel. We do not seek the answer we want to hear, we remain open to new views and ideas. Investigation prior to contempt is the key. We slow down and honestly contemplate the input we have received. We also go to our ultimate counselor, our Higher Power, and then meditate on the combined wisdom we have gathered.

I often share with my friends something like "Oh, by the way, if all five of your mentors independently give you the same input about an issue you are having, you can be pretty confident that you have the right answer." (This has happened to me on more than one occasion.) With the benefits of going through this process and the insight gained, we can move forward with much greater assurance that we are on the right path.

In summary, why wouldn't we get the advice and input of people who only want the best for us?

Given the effort and time it takes to build these types of relationships, and the needed investment to maintain them, there are only a small number of mentor relationships we can maintain at any one time. My recommendation would be no more than three to five. Although the building of these relationships takes commitment, the benefits received will far outweigh the investment we make.

Personal Story:

Michael had been miserable at his corporate job for a long time, feeling like he did not belong there any longer. In the last few years, things had gotten very difficult, as he was being asked to evaluate his staff time and time again and "select" those to be laid off. He had hired most of these employees and knew them well. Very difficult. He was only sleeping a few hours each night and drinking much too much coffee during the day. He was restless, irritable, and discontented, and constantly riddled with anxiety most of every day. He was starting to lose hope of ever being happy, joyous, and free again. Thoughts of engaging in any sort of addictive activities that might relieve the pain even for a short time came to him often.

He sought professional counseling, and that helped during the most difficult periods of the layoff cycles. However, one Sunday night he decided he had had enough and needed to reach out and get some new perspectives. So he called his sponsor who said, "Michael, why don't you just go to work tomorrow and act as if you had resigned, but then just go ahead and do the best you can on a daily basis." This idea somehow lifted a great burden. Michael also called his close friend, a retired pastor, who independently suggested he let go of his anxiety and instead pray to be directed for God's will to become clear. Michael spoke to a few others about this in a Sunday meeting, and they all pretty much said the same thing. After contemplating everyone's input and suggestions, he calmed down and regained a measure of confidence.

He went to his church shortly after, which was an Easter Sunday, and during the service, the pastor asked anyone who had problems in various areas, like their jobs, to fill out a prayer card and people in the church would pray for them for a month's time.

Exactly 30 days later, Michael was called into an executive's office, was told that his job was being eliminated, and that he had several options. Michael decided to leave, but was asked if he would stay for a few months to help with transition. This was an unusual request, since most people were asked to leave immediately when their positions were eliminated. He quickly agreed, and during the remaining months he had an opportunity to say good-bye to his coworkers and share stories with them of how God and his friends had helped him with his decision.

He often thinks back to that Sunday night when he was in great despair and of the still, small voice that quietly suggested, "Why don't you call someone?"

Where Do You Stand?

Question 1: Right now who is my mentor(s)? Is this relationship working for me?

Question 2: If I need mentors, whom could I ask, and why them?

Question 3: If I am unwilling to get a mentor(s), why?

Tool #10

It's sharing time
(Share your troubles and joys)

Classroom Wisdom:

"Trouble shared is trouble halved." —Dorothy L. Sayers

"I have learned now that while those who speak about one's miseries usually hurt, those who keep silence hurt more." —C.S. Lewis

"If we have no peace, it is because we have forgotten that we belong to each other." —Mother Teresa

10. It's sharing time
(Share your troubles and joys)

Tendency:

We like to keep things to ourselves. Someone asks, "How are you doing?" Our answer, "Fine." We may be suffering intensely on the inside, maybe due to holding on to a secret that is really making us miserable and the answer is the same: "Just fine." We resist opening up to others about our troubles, fears, insecurities, or needs. We perceive a risk of rejection, judgment, and/or implied weakness, which we strongly wish to avoid. We sometimes believe that what we have done, the thing we are so ashamed of, will be not be understood or accepted. Or, in another scenario, our pride and ego kick in, and we avoid talking about our problems, since we anticipate losing face, our reputation taking a hit.

For example, thoughts may go like this: "I have been in recovery for many years. I shouldn't be having this type of trouble, and, furthermore, I am past the need of sharing these problems openly with others. People will see this as a weakness in me and my program of recovery." Or, "This is embarrassing; I should be doing much better than this. Others have problems that are so much worse. It's okay to keep this between God and me." We fail to realize that by sharing our troubles in a spirit of humility, God may be able to use them to help others with similar problems.

Oddly, this secretive nature may also apply to good things and joys happening in our lives. We hesitate sharing these as well, since they may reveal parts of ourselves that might make us vulnerable. We ask ourselves, "Why should I share my life with others?" First, I seriously doubt they care; second, I'm probably just bothering them; third, my good fortune won't last long and I'll look foolish; and last, the more they know about me, the more open I am to hurt."

Recovery Tool:

We ultimately break through, open up, and share our joys and concerns with at least one person we trust. Many recovering addicts have three or four such confidants (see Tool #9 – Huddle Up). There is practicality in having several options, since any one person may be unavailable in times when we really need to communicate something personal. I have seen it many times when others have shared first with just one person, thinking that's the end of it, and then find themselves open to sharing the secret or problem with a larger group in their recovery community. It's like the saying goes, "Once the secret is out, it's not a secret anymore."

If we have a problem or issue, just talking to others about it will lessen the load and make us feel like we're not alone anymore. We may even get some practical feedback that will help in its resolution! We also tend to miss the fact that others may get as much from hearing about our situation as we get in telling it. So often I have heard these words, "Thanks for sharing, _____, it was just what I needed to hear to help me with a similar problem I was having." There is a saying in my recovery group that comes up very often in this context: "What comes from the heart, goes to the heart."

As our trust and faith in others grow, with important discernment about whom we can trust, we will tend to share more and more in an open, honest manner. Face-to-face communication is best; however, if that's not possible, a phone call works.

Personal Story:

Michael was having a problem at work. He was distraught and beating himself up with thoughts like, "This is such a small issue. Why can't I just deal with it and let it go?" He continued obsessing over the problem until, out of total frustration, he decided to go to a lunchtime meeting. On the way, he decided that he would talk about anything except this minor work issue. He thought, "I can't bring something like this up when so many people have 'real problems' in their lives. This would just be too embarrassing to raise as a problem." And so this obsessive, negative self-talk continued all the way to the meeting.

Once settled at the table, it was soon Michael's turn to share. He started to comment on the table topic and then stopped midstream and said, "I really had a problem at work this morning, and I need to talk about it." He went on to describe the issue and almost immediately felt relief.

After the meeting, a person Michael did not know came up to him and asked if he had a minute. He went on to let Michael know that he had experienced a very similar problem at work that day and was very grateful that Michael had shared the situation. He said it was exactly what he needed to hear. It had helped him understand that he was not alone obsessing with "small" issues like this, and also that it was okay for him to share these types of things at meetings.

Where Do You Stand?

Question 1: Do I typically share my troubles and joys with others? Why or why not?

Question 2: Where, and with whom, am I most comfortable doing this sharing?

Question 3: What troubles or joys in my life could I share right now?

Tool #11

Set your prisoners free
(Find ways to deal with anger and resentment)

Classroom Wisdom:

"Resentment is like taking poison and waiting for the other person to die." —*Malachy McCourt*

"For every minute you are angry, you lose sixty seconds of happiness." —*Unknown*

"Anger is one letter short of danger." —*Unknown*

11. Set your prisoners free
(Find ways to deal with anger and resentment)

Tendency:

At best, we are going to at least occasionally experience a certain amount of anger and resentment. This is true whether we are active in our addiction or are recovering. It is unreasonable to think we will ever totally avoid it. The anger or resentment may be directed toward anyone or anything, including God and ourselves. Further, the focus of our anger is not limited to the original "cause". It begins to spread, like a cancer, to many other situations and people in our lives. These can be very strong, emotional upsets that lead to a variety of problems for us.

To start, we experience a growing disconnection from God and others. Our spiritual connection begins to slip away, fading into the distance. Being in an angry, resentful mood, losing our spirituality, also triggers other defects to come flying out, e.g., selfishness, self-pity, pride, at times exploding, forcefully and destructively, affecting all those around us. With a quickly formed resentment, our attitude can change instantly from positive and friendly to extremely negative and nasty. We consequently lash out at others when they clearly don't deserve it, and our guilt for doing this further fuels our negative state.

Anger raises our blood pressure, causes insomnia, can give rise to heart attacks/strokes, and, turned inward, results in depression. If all of this isn't bad enough, if we stay in this resentful state for long enough, we may very well begin thinking about, or engaging in, relapse.

Recovery Tool:

It is a very difficult challenge to deal effectively with anger and resentment. Once we come to understand how often we develop resentments and allow anger to seep in, we begin to accept improvement in place of complete elimination.

First, we recognize and accept our feelings of anger and resentment. If we need to sort out our feelings to gain clarity, we call someone who really understands us. Then, as in all other problem areas, we ask God for help to release us from their grip. If we have caused harm to another human being, we ask them for forgiveness. These amends also include forgiving *ourselves* when we make mistakes or do things we are not proud of, so we can let go of the guilt and use the past only as a constructive tool for the future. If we have done something that we believe offended God, we tell Him so and ask His forgiveness. (Over time we are able to discern when amends are owed to others versus only to ourselves and God.)

After we have taken whatever restoration steps are needed, we strive to let go as best we can and *move on.* Do the next right thing, get productive, engage in something pleasant for us and for another human being. We can go for a walk, call a friend or mentor, go to a meeting, clean something, work out, go to a movie. We turn from our own thoughts to those who need help, as this is a powerful antidote to a primary defect: self-centeredness. If obsessive, negative thoughts return, *we can ask God to remove them . . . as many times as necessary.*

Tolerance and acceptance of others, including their defects, helps avoid or minimize resentments. We certainly need to protect ourselves from others' harmful behavior; however, viewing them as broken, ill people helps by giving us a different perspective regarding their apparent bad intent. We learn to understand and accept that *hurt people, hurt people.*

Remember that resentments are poison to us, hardened chunks of anger, generating negative emissions within our souls. These chains that keep our spirits bound are broken with forgiveness and tolerance, which allows us to once again experience some peace and serenity. We eventually realize that resentments definitely hurt us much more than those we resent.

I heard this prayer recently: *Bless them, change me!*

Personal Story:

Michael had been fuming at a colleague at work. The individual (John) had been rude and inconsiderate many times. He had made it clear that he did not like Michael and he was going to do whatever he could to get ahead of him in the company. Michael's ego was bruised; anger and resentment were in full bloom.

Michael began a long period of obsessive thinking, filled with plans of revenge and retaliation. He thought almost every day about the email he would write to John that told him where he was wrong, about the phone call where he would tell John what a real jerk he was, and so on and so on. He had angry dreams about John and spent many hours at work with his colleagues defending his position and trying to convince them that John was basically a bad guy. With John "renting free space" in Michael's head, Michael was not able to experience the peace and serenity available to him.

One day Michael described this situation to Sam, a friend in recovery. After listening for a while, Sam said, "I bet this John is having a great day today golfing, spending time with his family, enjoying life. No question in my mind that he has not thought about you for one second. By the way, how are you doing, Michael? "

"Not well," Michael responded.

Michael thought about this for a long time and finally realized that the real problem was his own. So he started, reluctantly, to do what he had been taught early on in recovery: pray for John every day, and then get to work on the things that were placed in front of him. He followed these actions for some time, and it began to relieve the anger and resentment. Michael reflected, "Another lesson learned, progress made."

Where Do You Stand?

Question 1: What anger and resentments do I have right now?

Question 2: What lingering anger and resentments are affecting me and my life? What is stopping me from letting go of them?

Question 3: When I rationally analyze my anger and weigh the costs and benefits, is it really worth it?

Tool #12

Tomorrow is another day
(Forgive yourself, release the past)

Classroom Wisdom:

"Realize deeply that the present moment is all you ever have. Make the Now the primary focus of your life." —Eckhart Tolle

"You can't undo anything you've already done, but you can face up to it. You can tell the truth. You can seek forgiveness. And let God do the rest." —Unknown

"If you have made mistakes ... there is always another chance for you ... you may have a fresh start any moment you choose, for this thing we call "failure" is not the falling down, but the staying down." —Mary Pickford

12. Tomorrow is another day
(Forgive yourself, release the past)

Tendency:

All of us come from a place where we did things we are not proud of, that made us sick in so many ways. We used and abused in order to do things we knew we shouldn't be doing, and then we had to use more to forget about what we had done. The cycle was relentless and endless. The more we acted on our impulses and answered the call of our addictions, the sicker we became and the farther we moved away from who God made us to be. Guilt and shame dogged us every moment of our existence, whether or not we were aware of it. We would quickly numb ourselves and rationalize in some distorted, dishonest way, what we were doing.

The harm we were doing to others was evident in their attitudes toward us; what was hidden in our denial was the damage we were causing to ourselves. Our very souls became figuratively blackened and hardened. We were, in essence, in a state of "hell on earth", even though we didn't know it or care to admit it. Living this way, we weren't about to forgive ourselves, since we were convinced there was no hope for change. And the addiction cycle continued . . .

Then came recovery and, with it, saner thinking. An increasing God conscience. A return to recognition of right and wrong; moreover, a growing and sometimes alarming awareness of the harm we had caused to ourselves and others by the way we had lived in the past. Without any more addictive behavior to mask these feelings of remorse and guilt, we experience the full effect of our actions. And it really hurts. We are in touch with all the pain, sometimes every minute and every hour of the day.

Recovery Tool:

One of the most basic tenets in recovery is the importance of ridding ourselves of guilt, shame, and remorse. If we don't, we will once again use or, at best, live a less-than-fulfilling life in recovery. The starting point for this type of healing is laid out in many spiritual and recovery principles: we clear the wreckage of the past and make amends to those we have harmed.

Once we have completed our amends, the guilt and remorse over our actions may remain even though we're confident we did the right thing concerning the injured parties. Why is that? Why didn't we reap the benefits of the amend step of action? The most likely answer is that we have not forgiven ourselves. We have not let go of the past. We are still hanging on to the feelings of guilt and remorse—of course we are, we know very well how to do that! We know how to exist in a state of muck and mire.

I have read and heard many times that our addiction wants us to stay stuck in this cruel, unforgiving state of mind. The more we beat ourselves up for our past sins and failures, the less likely it will be that we move on to a new life full of freedom and acceptance, a life where we don't have to engage in our addiction to escape reality.

What many of us have come to realize and accept is that we have and will at times continue to make mistakes that harm others and ourselves. However, we have a clear course of action when this happens: make amends and then trust that our God has forgiven us—*even if we don't feel like He has!* We forge ahead past our points of failure. We come to learn from our mistakes and work to make the changes necessary to avoid repeating them.

However, we eventually see the need to let the past go and move into the future with a clean slate on a daily basis. Most every day I do an inventory of my thoughts and actions and assess the negative **and** positive. Then I ask God to forgive my trespasses and with that move on to the new day the best I can. Only now am I understanding and accepting that what remains as guilt is my own self-condemnation. That's my issue. God is standing by ready to help us move forward.

Spiritual and religious people over the centuries have understood the need for forgiveness from God and have developed practices that help them remember God's grace. My friends and I have used some of these at spiritual retreats to help us recognize that God can and will forgive us if we ask. Some examples of these practices include: writing down our "sins" on paper and, with a personal prayer, throwing them into a fire, symbolically presenting them to God for his purifying cleansing. Or simply having a quiet time with God where we prayerfully acknowledge our faulty behavior and ask for His forgiveness.

Personal Story:

Michael had been free from his addiction for some time. However, negative thoughts about his past came often to his mind. "Boy, I really didn't do a very good job choosing and performing in a career for which I was suited. I could have been a very good teacher. When my sister came to the university I was attending to be with her big brother, I was way too busy partying to spend any time with her. Didn't get to spend much time enjoying my kids when they were little . . . Not feeling very good about the pain my first wife went through when I asked for and went through the divorce. Not very happy about leaving my wife and mother of my children to raise the kids pretty much by herself in those early years. Sure could have been a much better son and brother . . ." and so on.

Michael cried a bit upon these reflections, but did not use. After sharing these thoughts at many meetings and reading books on recovery, he gained some helpful insights. One thought was to leave the window of the past closed except for one little crack that he could peek through to help him avoid repeating the mistakes of the past.

Then came thoughts of the action steps he had taken already and the promises of recovery filled with hope. "Well, I made the best amends that I could to the women in my life. I call my family often now to talk with them and attend all our family functions. Heck, we recently even had an extended family gathering in a beautiful vacation spot. I am a good dad now, taking my son and daughter fishing, golfing, to ball games, and staying close with them as they meet the challenges of growing up. They have a safe home now where they feel very comfortable bringing their friends over. My wife and I read, talk, and pray together most every morning, reflecting on our lives together. I am able to start a new career now if I choose."

He thought, "Well, I'm finally on the right path now, better late than never. Thank you, God."

Where Do You Stand?

Question 1: Are there areas of my life where I have not forgiven myself? What is it that stands in the way? What would it take for me to allow myself forgiveness?

Question 2: Do I believe God has forgiven me for my past? Why or why not?

Question 3: If I believe God has forgiven me, and yet I have not forgiven myself, what does this mean?

Tool #13

Give yourself some TLC
(Take good care of yourself)

Classroom Wisdom:

"The name of the game is taking care of yourself, because you're going to live long enough to wish you had." —*Grace Mirabella*

"It is amazing how much crisper the general experience of life becomes when your body is given a chance to develop a little strength." —*Frank Duff*

"A good laugh and a long sleep are the best cures in the doctor's book." —*Irish Proverb*

13. Give yourself some TLC
(Take good care of yourself)

Tendency:

At times, we abuse our bodies, minds, and souls. We often let ourselves get **Hungry, Angry, Lonely,** or **Tired,** sometimes all of these at once. As the saying goes, we need to "halt" when we are experiencing any of the **HALT** symptoms. The reason for this is simple: while in any or all of these negative states, we are much more susceptible to addictive behavior.

Recovery Tools:

Exercise

A really powerful tool for achieving or regaining positive, mental health. Working out hard, in whatever way makes sense for you and your body, releases natural "feel gooders" in our bodies, positively and safely. I have found that exercise unquestionably reduces stress and improves my sleep patterns. We who suffer from depression are sometimes amazed at how rigorous exercise helps. And for those of us that are anxious, significant physical activity can often change our mood from negative to positive. Get a physical check-up before you begin.

Eat right

One day I was at a meeting and made this truthful admission in jest: "I'm not feeling well today. I wonder if it has anything to do with missing breakfast, eating a bunch of doughnuts, and drinking a couple of cokes for lunch?" A much better scenario for us is as follows (mom told me this a long time ago): We eat breakfast, lunch, and dinner and sometimes small snacks in between. We have a balanced diet of fruits, vegetables, fish, blah, blah, blah! It's frustrating, irritating, and not easy to implement, but so important for our physical and mental health. When we start eating healthily, we eventually feel better physically and thereby eliminate another potential source of our emotional and mental disturbances.

Sleep (Take a nap)

One day I called my sponsor and talked to him for a long time about my problems and issues (mainly those happening in my head). He didn't say a word. After I was done, he asked, "Are you tired?"

I said, "Yes." (I wanted to add, and what does that have to do with anything?)

He suggested, "Why don't you take a nap?" I did, and after I awakened, I completely understood the tool. I just felt calmer and less anxious. When we get tired, things always seem worse. One night I slept very poorly, woke up nervous and uneasy. I told my daughter this and she said, "Maybe you shouldn't watch those stressful television shows before you go to sleep." I stopped doing that and it helped. I slowly switched to a routine of doing peaceful things before I went to bed. Cut back on drinking coffee in the afternoon. Got some regular exercise. Started to go to bed at the same reasonable time each night. Read and listened to calm, spiritual material before falling asleep.

Result: I'm sleeping much better and can therefore eliminate poor sleeping from my inventory of negative contributors to my mental health.

Seek professional support

When I first got into recovery, the advice given to me went like this: haven't seen a doctor for a physical lately, have you? My answer, and I'm guessing this is true for many of us, was NO! Therefore, it was suggested that I find a general practitioner and then get a physical. I did this and have gone for an annual physical every year since. Same thing for a dentist. Only this is a twice-a-year drill. Do I look forward to these visits? No! Am I grateful I am able to do this? Yes! Do I benefit from taking care of myself in this way? Another yes! Simply put, it's just the sane thing to do.

Now for a more difficult area. During my recovery, there have been several points in time when I got stuck on something that was beyond the purview of my recovery groups, sponsors, and mentors. So off to a therapist I went. This willingness was triggered by a person with long-term recovery who asked this question, "Would it hurt you to go and try this?" The answer? No. Conversely, might it help? The answer? Yes. So why have contempt prior to investigation? I went to recommended therapists at several different points, and the results were clear. They helped get me over the hump. If spiritual/recovery tools are not working for certain areas in our lives, I just can't see why we wouldn't try pursuing outside professional help.

Get outside

Sunlight and fresh air help. A walk around a park with trees and flowers does something positive for our spirits and mental outlook. Walking on a beach or just looking out at a lake refreshes. Hiking in a forest lightens our moods and heightens our senses.

Doing these kinds of activities takes the focus off us and onto the wonders of nature.

Soft music and pleasant movies

I read once that King Saul of Bible fame would go through periods where he would become troubled, anxious, and rattled. I can relate. He would call in David (also of Bible fame) and have him play soft, peaceful music to calm him. This caught my attention, and I have tried it with positive results. I have a playlist filled with both spiritual and simple peaceful music that can really soothe my spirit at times. I find myself listening to this playlist more often and listening to my hard-driving rock and roll selections less and less. Same thing with my movie selections: the further along in recovery I get, the more I seek "feel-good movies" and the less I can tolerate violent, stress-filled, nasty-ending stories. Try peaceful, spirit-filling media to enhance your recovery.

Fun

In recovery, we can get into working to excess. We may try to make up for lost time by focusing on rebuilding our finances or trying to advance our careers in a frantic manner. Of course, like so many things, this can turn into an obsession. We are also focusing on rebuilding our relationships with family and friends, all of which are time consuming. Add to this the effort and time we spend building a solid foundation of recovery. So what happened to having fun and enjoying life, with its many exciting pastimes?

We need to add having fun to our life equation. Getting better includes enjoying things that bring us joy. To get started, try doing those things that made you happy, the simple things you really enjoyed prior to your addiction taking control of your life. For some reason, we tend to doubt that these activities from our past can ever be fun again. The belief that our addiction ruined them forever is not true. I, like many others in recovery, have tried and found that going back to the things we did for fun when we were "young" can bring us more joy than ever. What is it for you? Golfing, bike riding, hiking, fishing, gardening, traveling, movies, plays, model building, sewing, sporting events, family picnics?

Personal Story:

As part of the check-out from the treatment center, Michael was given a list of suggested activities to follow that were broad-based in nature. Wanting to take as much positive action as he could to help his recovery, he followed much of the advice given. He found a general doctor and began annual physicals. He found a local dentist and started getting regular check-ups. He began paying attention to what he was eating and made some progress in his diet. He started taking walks outside in the fresh air even though he'd much rather lie in front of the television.

He realized over time that some of the things he was watching on television and at the movies (many times into the late evening hours) did not do much good for the serenity he was seeking, nor was some of the music he was listening to, so he slowly let go of those.

Later in recovery he became aware of some deep-seated fears and anxieties that were blocking his way to peace. So he sought the help of a professional therapist and gained some powerful insights and tools for positive change.

All along this path of improvement, he began doing the things that he had enjoyed before his addiction stole their joy. One day he decided to return to the ballpark to which he had gone many times as a young boy. On the way to the game, he remembered the excitement and amazement he felt the first time he had walked up the gangway and saw the entire field come to life before him. That incredible experience had been lost during his years of alcoholism.

He wasn't sure what would happen when he returned sober. He walked up the same gangway and when he saw the field, tears of joy came. Michael just stood there and felt the joy and excitement once again; the gift had been returned to him through recovery and the grace of God.

Where Do You Stand?

Question 1: Do I take good care of myself? If not, why not?

Question 2: What could I improve in this area?

Question 3: What initial steps do I need to do to take action in this area?

Tool #14

Time to move forward
(The [your name] of old will use/abuse again)

Classroom Wisdom:

"By changing nothing, nothing changes." —Tony Robbins

"Getting over a painful experience is much like crossing monkey bars. You have to let go at some point in order to move forward." —C. S. Lewis

"God, grant me the serenity to accept the things I cannot change, the courage to change the things I can, and the wisdom to know the difference." —Dr. Reinhold Niebuhr

14. Time to move forward
(The [your name] of old will use/abuse again)

Tendency:

We resist change, even when we know it is good for us. When problems appear, we tend to look immediately toward people, places, and things in our lives as the source, thinking, in essence, that if these people or situations changed more to our liking, life would be so much better, maybe even perfect. The thought that what we really need to change is our thinking, attitudes, actions, and perspective usually escapes us.

After many years in recovery, I have concluded that change in ourselves—lasting, deep changes in the way we think and act—is one of the most difficult things in life to achieve. We fight change; our minds, wired with the comfort of knowing past experiences, resist change at every turn. We can wallow in our present state, since even though it's not a good place, we are comfortable there. As sad as it is, we understand who we are, rely on our damaging defects and weaknesses to get by, and, until our condition is unmanageable enough, do not hit bottom and get ready to move on.

We internally ask, "Why change when we don't have to? Why would we risk changing when we don't know what it will be like on the other side? Maybe we won't like the new situation or the new us. Oh, and by the way, why would I want to go through the pain and discomfort of making changes when I'm getting by just fine in my current state (of despair and unhappiness)? Who really wants to grow, compared to living in this comfortable (awful) existence?"

Recovery Tool:

Willingness is the absolute key to positive change. How willingness comes about happens in different ways. The most common change agent is intense pain. When the **current situation becomes more painful than the fear associated with the needed change**, surrender will happen and change will begin. Until that time it's very difficult to just say, "Oh, well, I guess I should stop doing this and instead do that. Okay, I guess I'll just start now." It is seemingly too difficult for us to help ourselves this easily. Sometimes the best we can do is to pray for the willingness to become willing.

Another change-producing catalyst that I have heard, seen, and felt is the power of prayer. I have experienced in myself (and heard others say in essence) that God changed my heart regarding an attitude or belief that I was unable to change on my own. We could not do it ourselves (somehow we always knew this to be true). However, when we prayed and God saw fit to prepare us for change, it happened with little or no struggle of our own. Some people refer to this as the "grace of God". Unwarranted merit. One explanation of why this can happen is that there is a grand plan, a master plan, and God is in charge. Whether we intend it or not, some changes will happen for the betterment of this world and us.

Like a mother giving birth to a child, the pain of change is inevitable, but from this pain comes the joy of . . . a new you.

Personal Story:

At a meeting Michael attended regularly, a good friend, George, would open his talk each time with this statement: "I'm here to change because the George of old will drink again . . . and this is where my professors are that teach me how to live."

At first, Michael would merely think that George's opening was pretty cool. It flowed nicely and went well with George's spiritual insights. Then as time went on, Michael came to deeply understand the power of the statement. If he continued doing, thinking, and acting in the same ways he did during his addiction, minus only whatever addictive device he used, he would surely find himself back in that awful hell on earth. He somehow understood that if he ignored the changes that were so clearly needed, he would be like a shark who tries to stand still in the water: he would suffocate and die. And he needed to surround himself with the "winners" in recovery, since they were the ones who knew how to "do sober".

So his only hope was and is to listen to those "professors" who abound in the recovery community and other spiritual venues, not only to hear what needs to change, but to become willing to take the necessary action to implement it in his daily life.

Where Do You Stand?

Question 1: How well do I embrace change?

Question 2: What areas in my life do I know I need to change?

Question 3: What changes do I find myself unwilling to make, why is this so, and what do I think it would take to become willing?

Tool #15

Seek and you will find
(Pursue spirituality)

Classroom Wisdom:

"We are not human beings on a spiritual journey. We are spiritual beings on a human journey." —Steven Covey

"I understand once again that the greatness of God always reveals itself in the simple things." —Paulo Coelho

"Spirituality is not about being fixed; it is about God's being present in the mess of our unfixedness." —Mike Yaconelli

15. Seek and you will find
(Pursue spirituality)

Tendency:

We addicts are constantly looking for comfort and relief, something that makes us artificially feel better. When we experience any type of negative emotions, like fear, depression, boredom, anxiety, or self-pity, our inner selves call for its immediate removal, the faster and easier the better. On the other end of the spectrum, when we feel good, resulting from success or good fortune, it's not enough. We addictively look for ways to increase the "rush". We are on a constant search for people, places, or things that make us feel less empty. We look for ways to get out of the restless, irritable, and discontented state in which we regularly find ourselves. We seek numbing solutions that will allow us to be comfortable in our own skins, for example, to sit peacefully and take in the beauty of life, a sunset, kids playing, dogs chasing a ball, or just a nice warm fire.

For those of us who are fortunate enough to get a moment of clarity, we one day realize that this spiritual, serene state for which we are deeply searching is not available through our addictive, compulsive actions.

When we pursued the wrong "fix" (addictive behavior) to take care of the void or pain, we simply ignored or shied away from any concern about the long-term negative effects of the addictive actions we were taking; we wanted what we wanted now, regardless of cost. The long-term cost was extremely high for us and those around us.

The major obstacles in gaining a natural, God-given state of serenity are that either (1) we don't know what the appropriate, healthy way is to get us there (tools), or (2) we do not have the willingness to take the necessary action required (do the work).

Recovery Tool:

I, like many recovering addicts, have found spirituality the foundation for addressing the most basic life questions. So how do we "pursue spirituality"? One of the most powerful ways is to ask God to just reveal Himself. Period. Requesting, in effect, if He is there, to show Himself in a practical, real way.

When I make this request of God, amazing spiritual things began to happen. It's like the saying goes, "When the student is ready, the teacher will appear." How will He appear? In many different ways. However, I have to pay attention. As a result, I see signs in churches that speak directly to my situation, stickers on cars that tell of God's love for me, ideas in books that help me today even though I had read the section many times before. I hear His care for me in church sermons, in 12-step meetings, and even from my wife and kids!

As time goes on, I also get healing guidance and comfort from hearing and discerning His still, small voice. And the corollary to this spiritual awakening, which is critical for growth, is: as was suggested to me, share these spiritual stories with others, no matter how small or strange they appeared.

For example (a real one), Hey, I was feeling really depressed and lonely today while driving to my appointment and asked God for help. I had the radio on, and for some reason started to focus on the words. The song was "You've got a friend". This changed my frame of mind immediately, as I spiritually discerned that this sequence of events was no coincidence.

Was this an answer to my prayer? I absolutely, without any doubt, say "yes". (If you get a chance, read the lyrics to that song and think about the scenario I described.) Another real example I experienced was just prior to getting into recovery. I pleaded with God to just leave me alone, to let me go my own way. I blurted out that I didn't need or want His help. Immediately after that "prayer", I "happened" to drive by a church sign that said, "You may be running from God, but He will not run from you". Seconds later, I looked at the car in front of me and the license plate said, "God loves you".

When I share these stories and many more that followed, what happened, and what typically happens, is that someone comments on the subject of spirituality and/or someone will tell a similar story of his or her own. I firmly believe that as long as we continue to share these stories, they will keep happening, resulting in spiritual growth in and around us.

Another powerful spiritual practice: "Be still and know that I am God" (Psalm 46:10, New Living Translation). Get quiet. Sit down, slow down, and calm down. Effective meditation can take many different forms. We find ways that work for us, and they probably will change over time. With the objective of quieting my mind and getting still with God, I have practiced many different tools that aid me. I read spiritual daily meditation books, rotating them over time. I listen to meditation tapes and practice daily journaling. Tracking, in writing, our spiritual growth in the form of character improvements and ongoing challenges allows us to see progress and to ask for guidance in specific areas. We can also record spiritual insights we have experienced. This is a form of journaling that many of us have found useful.

Be adaptable in the pursuit of spirituality. On vacations, I like to take in the natural surroundings, to appreciate the beauty and tranquility, and to "rest in them" in the knowledge that God is present. A couple of personal examples: when we visited the Grand Canyon, I was totally amazed at how long I could stare at the site and how spiritual it all seemed. I have the same type of experience every time I am blessed to be able to observe the power and vastness of the ocean. I have always felt these "touches of God" when visiting my favorite ballpark (hint: I live in Chicago) and when alone on a golf course at twilight. These are my own special connections with God. The important point is that each of us will find our own if we seek them.

Many addicts, including myself, have found spiritual retreats to be a great way of improving spirituality. A weekend surrounded with others, all who are seeking God, can do wonders for spiritual growth. The goal is to momentarily leave our life, with its problems and challenges, behind and take a long, peaceful "time out". Spiritual readings and movies are shared and discussed; long walks in the fresh air are taken, alongside a friend/mentor with whom we put our lives on the table. Spiritual topics are covered in the evenings, with the peace of a fireplace in the background. Stories of our journeys abound with laughter and some tears in the midst of a powerful fellowship of travelers on the road of recovery.

Finally, and simply, **help others**—a powerful path to spirituality.

Most of us eventually find the only solution to address our God-given spiritual void is to fill it with God-given spirituality.

Personal Story:

Michael was struggling to find a God that he could understand. He had heard all kinds of things to help him with this; however, they were not sinking from his head to his heart. He talked about the problem regularly at meetings. He just wanted to know that there was a God that cared about him in a real and practical way.

After one of these meetings, a friend of his in recovery suggested that Michael "challenge God" with a prayer that went something like this: "If there is a God, then show your face to me."

The next week Michael saw his friend at a convention, and with a face full of hope and joy, ran up to him with the following story:

Michael had said the prayer prior to driving to the convention. On the way there, he passed a very large billboard that had the following quote: "I don't question your existence, why do you question mine?" The quote was signed, "God."

Where Do You Stand?

Question 1: Do I consider myself to be on a spiritual path? Explain.

Question 2: Where and when do I best make spiritual connections? What additional things would I like to pursue in this area?

Question 3: What spiritual stories do I have that I could share with others?

Tool #16

Glass half full
(Make a gratitude list)

Classroom Wisdom:

"When we lose our gratitude, we gain a bad attitude." —AA saying

"What if all we had today was what we thanked God for yesterday?" —Author unknown

"Success is getting what you want; happiness is wanting what you get." —Ingrid Bergman

16. Glass half full
(Make a gratitude list)

Tendency:

One of the "features" of our addiction is thinking negatively. For so many of us, this is unfortunately a default state of mind. Without any effort at all, we easily find every flaw and "down side" of people, places, and things in our lives. When we think about our friends, family, where we live, our job, and the future, we are flooded with a consistent flow of negative scenarios. On many days, doom and gloom seem to be on every horizon. When we project, isn't it always a negative outcome that we forecast? Let's not forget that when we were engaged in our addictive lifestyle, at least part of this fear and projection of disaster had merit. We need only to reflect on the things we were doing as a result of our addictive patterns, and it becomes easy to understand why we predicted such bad results.

Even in recovery, we can have an internal blind spot regarding the amazing good and positive blessings that are present in our lives. When our family and friends try to remind us of these good things, we may disregard them or lash out in anger. We rob ourselves of happiness and joy by engaging in this self-defeating self-talk that has us believing things are much worse than they really are. We find ourselves constantly and obsessively dwelling on what we *don't have* instead of all the good things we *do have.*

I'm not sure why this is. Maybe it's the thinking pattern with which we were born, or developed over time, that played a part in our addiction. Maybe it came as a result of, or at least worsened through, our addictive and compulsive patterns. The reasons don't really matter. It is what it is. One thing is certain: dwelling in this state of mind leads us to bad places, potentially back to our addictions, back to the dark where light has a hard time getting in, "back into the shadows", as my friend Tony says.

Recovery Tool:

When we consider the impact of this negativity in our nature, we can easily understand how much better life would be if we could focus on the positive. In an optimistic, grateful state of mind, we experience moments of peace, periods of serenity. Through a willingness to change our actions and thinking, we begin to see our blessings. In whatever condition we find our family and friends, our health, our careers, our relationship with God—in other words our present—we are able to find a positive. The glass is half full, not half empty. Now that we are in recovery, on the right path, we sense that we have a much brighter future. We develop a hope for a better life to come and gratitude for our present recovery.

Eventually we hear the idea of keeping a gratitude list, and we do so. We begin to write down our blessings, and seeing them in black and white helps us further acknowledge their reality. We make these lists on a periodic basis, add to, and review them when the spirit moves us. I find it useful to take time out two or three times a year to reflect on the list. In times of self-pity, I am often prompted to take stock of these gifts in my life, lest I forget how fortunate I really am.

We find that, as our perspective on life changes for the better through recovery, a new inventory of positives emerges. Upon review, we will be surprised at how much we have taken for granted and how many blessings are present in our lives. Knowing and accepting that we will lose what we have on our list by returning to our addiction(s) serves as a realistic deterrent to relapse.

Even when our circumstances turn difficult, we can be assured that we will be able to deal with them in a sane and mature manner as long as we apply our recovery tools. That's positive. More and more I view bumps in the road, challenges, as opportunities to learn and grow. Do I like the pain of growth? No. Do I like to hear these words, "God is interested in our growth, not our comfort?"

Absolutely not. It's difficult to view troubles and difficulties with gratitude. However, if my goal is to be the person God intended me to be, then I must deal squarely with all that life brings.

We start by *"thinking what we are thinking about throughout the day"*. Then by consistently focusing our thinking on the potential for brightness and good in our futures, instead of doom and gloom, a difficult but needed change will happen. Why is it so hard to project positive instead of negative even when we have moved into a pattern of better living? Because we have spent many years training our brains to think negative thoughts. We practice replacing negative thinking with positive affirmations, like the serenity prayer or verses from the Bible or slogans from our recovery programs, e.g., "easy does it". This change in thinking patterns takes time; it typically happens slowly and requires a disciplined effort of positive thinking and actions. We look for daily progress.

We come to find that if we do the next right thing, the chances of good things happening are greatly enhanced. When we practice this simple but powerful principle, we start to expect and recognize the blessings that have and will come our way.

Personal Story:

Michael was talking with his friend, Tom.

Tom: "How are you?"

Michael: "Not doing very well today."

Tom: "What's up?"

Michael: "Well, I stunk out on the golf course today."

Tom: "Oh. So you were able to play golf today? You were able to take off work, had your own set of clubs, had friends that joined you, and felt healthy enough to walk the 18 holes?"

Michael: "Yes, but I really played badly."

Tom: "What else?"

Michael: "I hate my job."

Tom: "Oh, so you do have a good job that pays you well, with benefits? Anything else?"

Michael: "My wife and kids are really getting on my nerves."

Tom: "This is the wife that stuck with you during your addiction and the kids who are healthy and doing well? More?"

Michael: "Yep. I don't like the meetings I am going to. The speakers are boring, the topics are getting old, and the old members talk too long."

Tom: "These are the meetings that you went to that helped you get clean and sober? The meetings that you can drive to almost any time of the day when you are having problems? The people who sat with you for hours and listened to your junk?"

Tom left, shaking his head, clearly frustrated. Later that day after reflecting on the discussion, Michael wrote a gratitude list and thanked God for His kindness, care, and understanding for someone like himself.

Where Do You Stand?

Question 1: Does my default thinking tend to be negative? Give examples.

Question 2: For what and whom am I currently grateful?

Question 3: What actions can I take to maintain a grateful, positive mind-set?

Tool #17

Back to kindergarten
(Be honest and follow the rules)

Classroom Wisdom:

"The way out of trouble is never as simple as the way in." —*Edgar Watson*

"Integrity has no need of rules." —*Albert Camus*

"Honesty is the first chapter of the book of wisdom." —*Thomas Jefferson*

17. Back to kindergarten
(Be honest and follow the rules)

Tendency:

In our addictions, we regularly looked for ways to break the rules. We sought the easier, softer way to get what we wanted. We did dishonest things, both large and small. The criterion for evaluating our actions was simple: did we get caught (bad), or did we get away with it (good). We were indifferent to the effect of our actions on others.

It is interesting that, when breaking the rules, many addicts will tell you that deep inside they knew they were doing wrong. The longer we behaved in a dishonest manner, the less it bothered us and the easier it became to ignore any feeling of remorse. And, of course, as we continued in this way of living, our addictions increased, adding to the vicious cycle of guilt, shame, and unhappiness.

Early on in our addiction, we began lying to ourselves. We could not reconcile our actions as being the right thing, so we necessarily went into a state of denial, first rationalizing small things we were doing "to take care of ourselves", and then on to larger denials of behavior under the guise of "we deserve it". We lied to others in order to survive, or merely because it had become a natural behavior. With the way we were living, dishonesty became a requirement for survival. We were constantly looking behind us to see what we needed to cover up.

The result was that every time we lied or were in some way dishonest, it was as if another weight were added to our already troubled souls. Once again, our mechanism of coping: run as fast as we could to our addiction in order to escape from ourselves. As this type of life went on, we began to lose our true identity. By not being honest or genuine, along with our other addictive behaviors, we were walking down the path that lead to despair, lack of self-respect, and eventually a nasty bottom.

Recovery Tool:

It is so freeing to live an honest life where we make decisions dictated by our conscience, follow the rules, and tell the truth. It's much easier. We're not forced to constantly try to remember what we did and said, followed by new lies that keep us afloat. The notion that we must try to find a way to get past the gates for free, get to the front of the line without waiting, keep money given to us by mistake, etc., is viewed for what it is—cheating. Living by the rules and behaving honestly is a pathway to peace.

The interesting thing is doing the right thing may feel funny at first, as if we weren't taking care of ourselves. This feeling is just a transition place on the way to learning a new, better way of living. The opposite is true as well. When we do things in recovery we know are not right, we become uneasy, uncomfortable.

Even small improvements in this area help. For example, when we tell someone we will give them a call, or we will be at some function to support them, we do our absolute best to follow through with these promises. People notice. When we get the wrong change in our favor, we give it back. No reason to keep it, only to be forced to go back later and return it, due to a screaming conscience! Honesty, regardless of who else knows it, builds character and self-esteem.

In a related area, we start sharing helpful things with people, even when we know they won't like it. We find that in the long run, it's much better for them and us to lay it on the line as long as we have the right motive and attitude.

And it all starts with *being honest with ourselves*. We take responsibility for our thoughts and actions even when we would rather deny them away. No matter what we've done wrong, we understand that we must honestly accept where we have erred, so that we can move on, correcting our actions along the way. Following this approach, we can live life on a day-to-day basis and no longer drag the baggage of our past into the future.

Personal Story:

Michael was in a department store shopping. He was in a good emotional place, happy to be buying Christmas gifts for his family. As he began the check-out process at the register, he noticed the cashier was only charging him for every other item. "What are you doing?" he asked.

The cashier responded, "This is the last day I'm working here, so I'm giving you this early Christmas gift." Michael's stomach immediately began to hurt.

A thousand thoughts seemed to pass through his mind in a moment, the last ones being the strongest. They were the ones that pushed him into action: "If I let this happen and walk away from here, I will be at home, feeling guilty, disconnected from spirituality, and, most assuredly, restless, irritable, and discontented. Then I will need to call my sponsor and tell him what I had done. He definitely will tell me to bring the items back and pay for them so I can get out of this funk. Then, I will need to go back to the store and admit what had happened and, in essence, make amends for my actions."

With this scenario playing out fully in his mind, he said to the teller, "Stop what you are doing and start again from the beginning, and please charge for all the items." The teller was stunned. "Whatever," he replied, somewhat irritated, and did what Michael asked.

Michael left the store feeling very good about his new way of life.

Where Do You Stand?

Question 1: What does "follow the rules" mean to me?

Question 2: Do I tend to follow rules in recovery? Is this important?

Question 3: Where do I need to be on guard in this area?

Tool#18

Please wait to be seated
(Have patience)

Classroom Wisdom:

"Patience is the ability to idle your motor when you feel like stripping your gears." —Barbara Johnson

"Patience and perseverance have a magical effect before which difficulties disappear and obstacles vanish." —John Quincy Adams

"Rivers know this: there is no hurry. We shall get there some day."—A. A. Milne

18. Please wait to be seated
(Have patience)

Tendency:

We are impatient people. We want what we want, when we want it, and "in a minute" is not fast enough. With this demanding attitude, our addictions flourished. Driven by extreme willfulness, we force things, ignoring signs that this may not be the right answer or the right time. We jump ahead blindly without asking questions or examining options. We are impulsive when we should be thoughtful and thorough. Go fast and we won't have to feel the discomfort of waiting; that's what we think and feel. When people don't call us back immediately, we get irritated and resentful. Don't they know we want to talk to them right now? When we point something out to our family asking for a change, we expect that they will accept this without discussion and implement our demands immediately. When this doesn't happen—boom! Another "justified" resentment.

Even though our family, friends, and colleagues may be preoccupied, tired, or in a bad mood, we force issues with them anyway, because now is a good time for *us*. We pray and ask God for things, good things that are aligned with His will for us, and we don't understand why we must wait for an answer. We just won't accept the answer from Him being **no** or **wait**. At times, we do want to grow and get better; we see the things in us that need to change, but then get frustrated and disheartened when change comes ever so slowly. In our ideal, unrealistic world, everything that needs conclusion must be resolved right now.

By nature, patience and tolerance do not come naturally to us. On a regular basis, our timing just stinks; "mere" progress toward our goal is seen as less than enough.

Recovery Tool:

We wait patiently. We don't force things. We think things through before we act. We deal with the discomfort of an unfinished matter and know that when the time is right, we will calmly move into action. We have confidence that in God's world, all things are woven into His master plan and in the perfect time frame. A good friend of mine talks about things happening in "God's calendar". We strive to seek and align with His timing, find this rhythm, and go with the flow of it. We can ask others for their thoughts on timing; we can get quiet with God and seek His direction. We can wait for things to *feel right* in our spirit . . . and once this happens, move forward confidently. We *trust* that things will work out well, when the time is right.

We are patient with our recovery and ourselves. When we are on the right path, we will grow, grow in the right direction. However, growth does not imply a straight line upward. We will make mistakes; we will revert to old ways at times. Learning from our mistakes, being kind to ourselves, and then moving forward is our formula for making progress. Continuing to dwell on our past mistakes doesn't help. Instead, we pick ourselves up off the ground and begin moving again toward our goal. Change, especially major changes in our beliefs and attitudes, takes time.

We wait patiently for answers to come for small and large problems. We seek advice from others and ask God for direction and insights. Then we stay alert for a spiritual response to our situation. The life lessons will take different forms. The insights we need may come from a friend, family, or mentor, may be discovered in a book or song, or even a sign along the road.

We "let go and let God", especially in the area of needed change within ourselves. God performs the change. We do the footwork, avoiding things that He reveals are not good for us, and taking action on the things that will help us. *We cooperate with God.* However, He is the master craftsman of the change; peace comes when we eventually realize and accept this.

Personal Story:

Michael was new to recovery. He had just joined a recovery group where they discussed the 12 steps each week. Members of the group varied in terms of how long it took for each of them to get through all the 12 steps. Typically all the steps were completed within a six-to-12-month period.

At the first meeting Michael attended, the discussion was heavy with resistance from some of the members who were being asked to move forward with the 12 steps. Without delay and with bold intention, Michael made this statement, "I'm ready to do all the steps as quickly as possible. One a day or one a week is fine with me." (He had privately concluded that, with his education and intelligence, he could get through these steps much quicker than others in the room!)

The consensus of the group was that Michael should focus only on the first three steps until further notice. Michael experienced immediate resentment and frustration. "How dare they," he thought. However, he was ready to listen and follow direction, since he had nowhere else to turn. After six months or so, Michael shared the following: "You guys were right. I'm doing just fine on the first three steps and will continue to work them for some time to come." Without much hesitation and almost simultaneously, several members responded, "Begin the fourth step immediately!" Everyone laughed, and Michael understood.

Michael was new to the idea of waiting patiently. But he found out through working the steps of the program that this was a glaring defect. He reports that some progress has been made, but it has come slowly. Michael still smiles when he remembers his friend Ed's constant joke, "I prayed for patience, and God responded by putting a 100-car freight train in my path! Be careful what you pray for."

Where Do You Stand?

Question 1: Am I a patient person? Explain, give examples. What would others say?

Question 2: Am I tolerant of others? Explain, give examples. What would others say?

Question 3: What can I do to improve in these areas?

Tool #19

Boot camp
(Practice self-discipline)

Classroom Wisdom:

"There are no shortcuts to any place worth going."—Beverly Sills

"In the confrontation between the stream and the rock, the stream always wins – not through strength, but through persistence."
—Buddha

"Discipline is the bridge between goals and accomplishments."
—Jim Rohn

19. Boot camp
(Practice self-discipline)

Tendency:

Most of us were, at least at times, lazy, selfish, irresponsible, and lacking in discipline. The "at times" part of this statement is most likely kind. It is very easy to get into narcissistic, pleasure-driven bad habits; this takes no effort or struggle at all. We excessively and compulsively smoked, drank, ate, gambled, watched television, played video games, etc., without any effort or discipline required! The more we engaged in negative habits and routines, the farther we were removed from becoming healthy, balanced, and effective people.

These undermining practices lulled us into a self-centered state and created a growing barrier to our source of real power—God. Why did we fall into this trap? I believe it's the result of habits ingrained over time and our default nature, which constantly demands immediate gratification with minimal effort. With our addictions giving us these temporary and self-defeating "rewards", i.e., fleeting, artificial pain reduction, we quickly and easily submit to them repeatedly; and so they become habit. And habits accompanied by obsessions are hard to break. So hard, in fact, we usually cannot break them through our own willpower.

When it comes to positive actions like exercise, working the steps of recovery, taking a daily inventory, meditating, going to meetings, socializing, reading helpful books, calling on others when we need help, etc., we struggle to find the willingness. These positive, "good habits" are difficult to start and require constant vigilance to keep them as a regular practice in our lives. Good habits and disciplines take effort, willingness, a conscious desire to change for the better, and the power of God to help us embed them into our lives.

Recovery Tool:

Practice, practice, practice! We ask God for help. We do the next right thing in terms of healing and maintaining our body, mind, and spirit. We implement, through a disciplined attitude of willingness, good practices and habits; soon they become part of our routine. We do not feel right if we don't do them once they are fully embedded in our lives. It's okay if we are not perfect at this—we won't be. Remember, progress, not perfection. When we "backslide" here, we pick up and engage in healthy practices again. We learn and move forward.

On the other side of the coin, we ask God to eliminate *all* the bad habits that hinder our growth. Over time, we become increasingly aware of what these negatives are and why they are not good for us. We pray for the willingness to let them go until they lose their power and attraction. Over time, the pain and discomfort of engaging in these defects will be greater than the temporary escape they tempt us with. The interim void we feel when finally letting them go will also dissipate.

We talk to our mentors about our commitment to new and healthy practices (at least the major ones), and ask them to hold us accountable in following through with our action plans. When the going gets tough, we get into action: attending extra meetings, praying, picking up the phone, helping others, etc. It's amazing how the rest follows. When the nose of the camel is in the tent, chances are the rest will come along.

Personal Story:

Linda entered recovery with very little self-discipline and lots of bad habits. She was immediately given a set of specific actions to get her going in a positive direction. It was suggested that she ask God for help immediately upon waking, and at the end of the day thank him for her sobriety. She was told that it was a good idea to go to a recovery meeting every day until she liked them and then keep going. After a year of sobriety, it was suggested that it would be good for her health if she stopped smoking. She went back to church each Sunday on a regular basis. She began working out and watching the food she ate. She eventually stopped smoking; and she spent less time compulsively buying things that were not really needed and starting saving some money.

After working the 12 steps of recovery year after year, they became part of her everyday living. She was able to pay special attention to specific steps at times of need, instead of merely obsessing about her problems.

All in all, Linda has achieved a level of self-discipline she never thought possible, and many bad habits have been lessened or eliminated.

Where Do You Stand?

Question 1: What does being a disciplined person mean to me?

Question 2: In what areas am I disciplined? How did I gain this discipline?

Question 3: In what areas do I need more discipline? What actions can I take to gain this?

Tool #20

Walk before you run
(Seek progress, not perfection)

Classroom Wisdom:

"Be not afraid of growing slowly; be afraid only of standing still."
—*Chinese proverb*

"Success isn't how far you got but the distance you traveled from where you started."—*Steve Prefontaine*

"I might not be where I want to be, but thank God I'm not where I used to be."—*AA Slogan*

20. Walk before you run
(Seek progress, not perfection)

Tendency:

Done with the right attitude and motives, reflection on our failings and defects is productive and allows us to grow spiritually. However, holding on to guilt and remorse is not constructive or healthy. Just like our approach to many things, we take the concept of being hard on ourselves to the extreme. One mistake and our day is a total disaster. One error and we begin the negative thought pattern that takes us to believing we are not a capable or worthwhile person. One flaw or defect we discover in our personality can overshadow all the good we recognize in ourselves.

The reality is, the saner and healthier we become, the more we can see how far from perfection we are. We make progress a negative as opposed to a realistic, affirming positive. Continuing the self-inflicted beating, we look at our past life, when addictions flourished, and shake our heads with disgust and remorse at the damage we caused. This constant battering of our inner selves takes a toll. If we stay in this condition, we open ourselves up to relapse or, minimally, a life void of the joy, happiness, and contentment available to us.

A related result of this harshness turned inward is that many times we extend this expectation of "perfection or else" to those around us. Why are they not perfect either? Why can't they see the flaws they have and fix them? If they won't let me fix them, maybe I should just find new friends, or a new family who surely will have fewer issues. The more we don't like ourselves and the things we do, the more easily we project this condition to others around us. They, of course, respond negatively, and the downward cycle for all continues.

Recovery Tool:

We remember that, although we addicts are imperfect, recovering people, we are doing the best we can to get well. We realize that all human beings have flaws, make mistakes, and have done things in the past they are not proud of. The tool here is well captured in the saying, "seek progress, not perfection". Having this goal keeps us moving in the right direction, with realistic expectations. Every day we objectively review our mistakes or failings, and then ask God to forgive them. Tomorrow we will once again seek continued improvement and change.

In addition, and with an equal degree of focus and honesty, we look at the positive actions we take each day (especially when they involve change) and thank God for those as well. These positive fruits of sobriety are making us and our lives better: "better" defined as moving toward becoming a person we actually come to like and respect, one whom we can live with in peace and acceptance. One day after many years of recovery, I looked in the mirror and thought, "You know, I really am getting better. I don't love me yet, but I don't hate me anymore either. Maybe I'm not such a bad guy. Maybe there is hope for me after all!"

On the subject of healing and positive growth, it is very common that others see positive changes in us before we do. I have heard countless stories (which always trigger smiles and feelings of gratitude) of recovering addicts who tell of mothers, fathers, spouses, and children who, with tears of joy, thank them for their sobriety. They have been given a priceless gift of new hope for the future, of a possible and necessary ending of the pain and dysfunction of living with an active addict. This type of "family recovery" always takes time and isn't without bumps along the way. But just like a stone thrown into a pond, the healing of recovery starts with the addicts and then ripples out to those in their lives.

Personal Story:

Michael described at a meeting how he had found a simple tool to objectively evaluate the progress he was making. The tool is a daily inventory completed on a sheet of paper with two column headings. On one side of the paper is a plus (+) sign and on the other a minus (-). He described that over time, the definition of what each column heading meant had changed. Here were some of the column definitions he had used over time.

(+) What did I do today to keep me on a sober path? (-) What did I do that got me closer to a drink (the old me)?

(+) What did I do today that pleased God? (-) That made Him sad?

(+) What did I do today that made me feel good about myself? That improved my self-respect? (-) What did I do today that didn't make me feel good about myself?

(+) What did I do today that got me closer to being the person God wants me to be? (-) Farther away from that goal?

Within these categories, he considered his actions and thoughts for the day. Improvements and continual issues in areas such as selfishness, self-will, anger, resentment, relationships, trusting God, fear, etc., were listed, and reflected upon, and accepted as part of the reality of that day.

When Michael first heard about this tool, he immediately concluded that he would run out of space on the negative side and have little to add to the positive column. He found out fairly quickly that this was not true. Each day he had no trouble identifying areas in which he was improving, areas in which he was making progress. After reviewing a year of these daily records, it was clear he was getting healthier, becoming a much better person on the inside as well as in his actions toward the world as a whole. On the negative side, he saw how certain defects had a recurring cycle. He realized that to grow further and achieve a new level of peace and serenity, he needed to become willing to give these "chains" to God and let them go.

In the final analysis, he thought, "I am not perfect by any means, but, man, I'm sure getting better."

Where Do You Stand?

Question 1: How do I see myself making progress? Examples?

Question 2: In what ways do I tend to beat myself up for mistakes? Get frustrated and resentful at the flaws of others?

Question 3: In which areas would I like to focus on making more progress?

Tool #21

Fill the void
(Discover God)

Classroom Wisdom:

"God could and would if He were sought." —AA Slogan

"Just as a candle cannot burn without fire, men cannot live without a spiritual life." —Buddha

"Trust in the Lord with all your heart; do not depend on your own understanding. Seek his will in all you do, and he will show you which path to take." —Proverbs 3: 5-6

21. Fill the void
(Discover God)

Tendency:

So many times, and in so many ways, I have heard addicts describe their version of a void or hole in their souls that they tried desperately to fill. It's an empty feeling, one that has us sensing that there is something missing, that we are less than complete. This spiritual void drove us on a constant and urgent search for a solution. Was it a pill, a drink, a selfish relationship? Something, anything that made us feel artificially better; took the edge off; got us temporarily comfortable in our own skins. The easier and faster it was to engage in, the better.

During times when we are disturbed, fearful, or, alternately, full of pride and ego, this spiritual vacuum seems especially insatiable. No matter how much addiction we poured into our God-built spiritual place, e.g., money, sex, shopping, gambling, alcohol, drugs, etc., it wasn't enough. Our "false gods" just couldn't do it. They never will. Not only did these temporary "fixes" fail to fulfill our spiritual needs, they progressively destroyed our lives as they demanded more and more of their consumption, an increasing amount of "poison" just to allow us to exist in a miserable and worsening state.

Continually and progressively, like a python slowly wrapping its death grip around our bodies to suffocate and kill us, these addictions sucked life itself out of us. Our journey on this Earth was never meant to have this type of despair and misery.

Recovery Tool:

We find, over time, that there is only one solution to filling our true spiritual needs. Only one thing fits a perfect design to fill the void. *The missing piece* is the spirituality of a personal relationship with God on a daily basis. Discovering this spirit-filled way of living is a life-long journey. It takes time and effort to build a personal relationship with God, exactly in the same manner as it takes to develop any relationship. We seek to know Him and his ways. We learn that He is not a "candy dispenser"—giving us what we want as a spoiled child continually whines for. He also is not a cruel punisher of bad deeds. He will guide and direct us (*if we let Him*) to the thoughts and actions that are good for us, those that are aligned with His will for us, for a better life, which He wanted for us from the beginning.

We communicate with Him and learn His ways, as a child from a loving parent. We ask simple prayers: please help, please take these thoughts away, please help me stay clean today, come with me into this difficult situation, etc. And then we thank Him for what He has done for us. We discover those things that feed our spirits in healthy and positive ways. We help others, we engage in regular, quiet meditation, we take inventory of our actions, we are kind to those around us and ourselves, we journal, we spend time in nature, we continually read, listen, and learn about God.

When we are aligned with His will and follow through on His direction coming to us through many sources, our spiritual needs begin to be met. When we seek spiritual understanding and move into action on what is revealed, incredible results follow. Our spiritual emptiness begins to fill with the right stuff, good stuff, and the *resulting effect is that our compulsive, addictive cravings subside.*

I have experienced this many times, and it always strikes me that this place I get to (when I am really in sync with God) is exactly what I was searching for when I pursued substitute addictive alternatives. The ability to sit in a chair, watching a child at play, peacefully enjoying a beautiful sunset, listening to birds sing in the springtime, *and feeling at peace with the world* is an experience that represents heaven on earth for many of us. This state of contentment, gratitude, serenity, of being at peace with God, the world, and myself is . . .

I can't come up with the words to describe it. If you have felt this, words are not needed. Tears fill my eyes as I even think about this unwarranted blessing.

A final observation on filling our spiritual holes with "God stuff": not only do our lives get better (surely on our insides), the lives of those around us improve as well. We slowly stop destroying our internal world and, as a result, everyone around us benefits. This is the nature of leading a spirit-filled life.

Personal Story:

Michael was new to the subjects of spirituality and God. He had been taught some things about the God of the Bible at church and at home when he was growing up, but this seemed like a lifetime ago. He had what is called "head knowledge", an understanding of religious concepts, but he didn't feel anything in his spirit. He didn't really know God through a personal connection with Him.

He did, however, have a group of recovering friends who talked regularly about the reality of God in their lives. This was interesting to Michael, since many of these people did not have any religious background. But they spoke of talking with God all day long, seeing His hand in many small things during the day, like a parking spot opening up so they could get the kids to school on time, or a call from their sponsor just at the right time, a job position that came their way when they desperately needed it, a tire that blew out just after coming off the highway . . . the stories went on and on. The more the stories were told, the more these "God coincidences" seemingly occurred.

Michael was preparing for a presentation to the executive board of his company. He was extremely anxious and projected a negative outcome. Nothing seemed to calm him, and time seemed to stand still. Not knowing what to do next, he called his sponsor who, although not familiar with the business world, had strong spiritual insights. He provided the following suggestion for Michael: "As you walk into the meeting, ask God to walk in with you and help you with the presentation."

All board members were present and seated at the conference table as Michael entered the board room. However, one very noticeable thing caught Michael's attention: directly across from where he was to be seated was one empty chair. Without much thought or hesitation, Michael asked His God to sit in that chair and help him. He immediately felt a peace come over him, which he knew was from a power outside himself. During difficult parts of the meeting, Michael would gaze over at the chair and gain needed strength and courage to continue.

After the presentation, Michael's superiors commended him on his poise and professionalism. Michael just smiled and responded both privately and vocally, "Thanks." Especially in times of fear and uncertainty, Michael continues to invite God to walk alongside him.

Where Do You Stand?

Question 1: Do I believe I have a built-in spiritual void?

Question 2: How have I tried to fill this void in the past?

Question 3: What do I believe are the right things that will truly fill the void? Which one(s) am I presently practicing? What further actions do I need to take for my spiritual growth?

Tool #22

Walk the balance beam
(Seek balance in your life)

Classroom Wisdom:

"The key to keeping your balance is knowing when you've lost it."
—Anonymous

"Happiness is not a matter of intensity but of balance and order and rhythm and harmony." —Thomas Merton

"Be moderate in order to taste the joys of life in abundance."
—Epicurus

22. Walk the balance beam
(Seek balance in your life)

Tendency:

Maintain balance in your life, a simple concept. Difficult to achieve for those with addictive personalities. We hear people making statements and asking questions surrounding balance all the time: "I can't stop eating them once I start." "How much service work should I do versus spending time with my family?" "Should I go to a meeting three times a day or do something fun with my family once in a while?" "Should I spend all of my time helping others, or should I work 12 hours a day, seven days a week to clear up my financial wreckage?" "If I enjoyed going to the movies last night, does that mean I should go the next three nights in a row?" "Is it okay if I only sleep five hours a night so I can work out seven days a week, or is that obsessive?" "How many people should I sponsor? one? five? 10? 20?" "It's probably not good that I drink 12 cups of coffee a day, right?"

Having to constantly deal with this issue myself, I continue to fight my all-or-nothing personality. If I were told to focus on just one thing, all the time, oh, my life would be so much easier! Like, "Forget about your finances, just take care of your health. Or "Sponsor all the people who ask you, your family will do fine without you while you do this." How about, "Make all the money you can now that you're sober; your recovery work can come later." Doesn't sound good, does it?

The missing elements are the concepts of balance and moderation. Simple wisdom, but oh so hard for addicts to incorporate in their lives. We think in black or white; grays do not apply to us. Our addictive personalities tell us that to stop in the middle, unfinished, to leave some of "it" for tomorrow, is not right, incomplete. Finishing it at some "later date" has no appeal.

We typically forge on, while our addictive personalities are "turned on", knowing we should stop, but without the power or willingness to do so. Forget about what other things we should be doing for others or ourselves. We hang on to the misconception that we know what's best for us, that we can handle it. The "more-is-better" pattern is a clearly destructive symptom of our addictive natures. So we are on the same page with this, just recall how we behaved while we were in the midst of our addictions. Did we ever easily stop using or engaging in our obsessions before they or we were completely exhausted?

Recovery Tool:

Yep, you got it. More is not better. A little of this, some of that, a bit of the other thing. Time with the family, time at work, time spent in recovery activities. A little golf, fun in the sun, projects at home, time with your sponsor, time with those you sponsor, time with the family. A piece of cake, not the whole thing. Some chips, not the whole bag. A few M&Ms, not the entire bag. Some time at prayer and meditation, some time at the movies. Talk with your spouse, walk in the park, do projects at home. Enjoy what you are doing, and when the time is *naturally* over, move on to the *next thing* without holding on to the *last thing*. We let go of the drive to excess and gradually accept that doing the next right thing, in the moment, is what gradually brings balance into our life. We finally learn that more is not better. And how the heck are we supposed to figure out when enough is enough and when we're "in balance"? How do we know? Answer: we learn over time. First, of course, by trial and error. For example, practice new skills, like letting go when we don't want to but know we should. Second, talk with others about this issue. Ask them what they think about your practices and perceived excesses.

(Just to be clear, this moderation principle does not apply to our addictions. With these, it's total abstinence.)

We learn that the balance equation is ever changing over periods of time or seasons. For example, when our kids were young, my wife and I allocated much of our non-work time to them. Early in recovery, I spent much of my free time immersed in recovery activities. Later as my career responsibilities grew, I spent longer periods of time working. And so on, and so on.

And, as always, communicate with your Higher Power. Ask Him to show you when you should stop and when you should start. He will give you a new sense of awareness of what to do and when. Try it. Put Him to the test. At some point, we will begin intuitively understanding what to do and when. What if we fall into excess in some area and "overdo it"? We acknowledge, accept, and learn from the experience. Then we can "fast" from whatever it is for a while until we achieve balance once again.

Personal Story:

Michael was still at the office. He had started the day at 7 a.m. and now it was 6 p.m. He was tired and stressed, but he had many open tasks he wanted to finish. It wasn't critical that he complete them that night. However, he just wanted to get a few more things done before he went home. "Finishing all of this is a good thing," he thought, "good for my career, very positive." He was hungry, so he ate a chocolate bar and had his fifth cup of coffee of the day. After working another three hours, he decided to go home for the evening. When he got home, his kids were already asleep; he ate a large meal, the first one of the day, and mindlessly watched television for a couple of hours, and then tried to go to sleep. Tired as he was from the hectic day, it took him a few hours to finally fall asleep, and after what seemed like just a quick nap, it was 6 a.m. and time to get ready for work.

On Saturday, Michael went to play golf to relax. He started at 7 a.m. with his dedicated golf partner, and by 5 p.m., they had played 61 holes of golf. He was tired and hungry, but he looked over at the first tee and said, "Hey, we could get one more hole in? How about it"? His partner, stunned by the question, tiredly replied, "I quit, I'm going home." Michael reluctantly left, got home late, and had doughnuts for dinner. He was exhausted and crashed until 10 a.m. the next morning.

Later that morning, his wife asked if he would spend some time with her and the kids at the zoo, and he responded, "Hey, I'd really like to, but I haven't been to a meeting in a while, and I'd like to go to three today to catch up. I also should call my sponsees and see how they are doing. Getting hold of all of them will take some time. Maybe next weekend we could do something."

Michael had heard of the concept of balance, but hadn't begun to practice it. It had not quite sunk in.

Where Do You Stand?

Question 1: Where am I with balance in my life right now? Explain.

Question 2: What areas are out of balance? What actions can I take to achieve balance?

Question 3: With whom can I discuss my life balance?

Tool #23

No more Mr. Scrooge
(Don't be so selfish, help others!)

Classroom Wisdom:

"One of the greatest diseases is to be nobody to anybody."
—Mother Theresa

"We work on ourselves in order to help others, but also we help others in order to work on ourselves." *—Pema Chodron*

"That which we do for ourselves we take to our graves, that which we do for others in this world lives on for eternity." *—Arthur Pine*

23. No more Mr. Scrooge
(Don't be so selfish, help others!)

Tendency:

Selfishness and self-centeredness may very well may be the most defining and negative trait of addicts. We see things happening to and around us mainly from the perspective of how they will affect *us*; in other words, what will it mean to *me* when or if something happens or doesn't happen? Looking at situations from another's point of view does not happen naturally or easily to people with our disposition, let alone looking at these situations with an empathetic attitude. Giving to others, especially those things we hold dearly for ourselves, is extremely difficult. This would include our money, time, energy, and support, or maybe just a timely compliment, a listening ear, etc.

In a related vein, we often demand more than is due to us. When something good comes our way, it is not enough—we want more, and then our compulsion to keep doing or using drives us to even greater excesses.

Selfishness and self-centeredness are recognized as a major source of trouble for people who suffer from addictions.

Recovery Tool:

We help someone. Really, anybody will do. They do not have to be in recovery. We give away things that we'd rather hold on to. When someone is hurting or suffering, we are attentive to their needs. We give money to charities and to those in need. We take the time to listen attentively to someone who is hurting without rushing to give them a suggestion or advice. We figuratively "lean in" to hear them better. When we ponder why God has given us so many undeserved blessings, we come to see that, at least in part, it may be so we can be of service to others. We eventually realize that we are blessed so we can bless others. Small things count. Helping others in need is completely and purely aligned with God's will and His purpose for us.

Eventually a strong desire to give to others what we have been freely given emerges within us. Many of us engage in what can be broadly defined as "service work". We do many of these service-related activities within our 12-step programs of recovery, e.g., chair meetings and speak, sponsor others, serve on committees, drive newcomers to meetings, make coffee and set up tables, etc.

Other types of service work that are fulfilling to our spirits include feeding the poor and homeless, volunteering in nursing homes, taking care of the ill and physically challenged, visiting those in jail and the hospital, and going to wakes and funerals. Even picking up a piece of garbage or putting a shopping cart back provides a service to God and those around us. All of these activities get us out of ourselves and make us useful instruments for implementing forces of good in this world; they also have the decidedly positive effect of quieting our addictions.

We come to find that there is an important distinction between being selfish and taking care of yourself. We learn to take care of our mental, physical, emotional, and spiritual health, which puts us in a good position to effectively help others. We need God's help, sometimes spoken through the counsel of others, to distinguish when it's time to take care of ourselves and, conversely, when we must turn away from ourselves and focus on the needs of others.

Helping others is a pathway to positive living: happiness, good health, and humility.

Personal Story:

Michael was on his way to drop his kids off at day care. He was in a rush, as always. The kids were a handful, but Michael was dealing with it as best he could—no alcohol or drugs to numb reality. He got them through the revolving doors and hurried down the hall. However, as he glanced to his left, there was a woman with a baby stroller who was clearly having difficulty getting through the doors. Michael thought, "Yeah, I see her, but, hey, I'm in a hurry to get my kids to school so I can get to work." However, after a few more steps, he stopped in his tracks. He just could not ignore the person in need. He helped her through the doors, and once outside, the mother looked directly at him and said a simple, "Thank you so very much."

Michael went on to work, but for a week or so things were different. He kept thinking about the person he helped and how so important that one simple act was for him. He pondered over this at length, since he couldn't quite understand why such a small thing meant so much. As time went on, the answer came. Helping people does not have to come in the form of some major event, like giving away a million dollars to charity. Just one small act can make a world of difference to someone.

Open the door for a mother and child, visit someone in the hospital or jail, listen to someone who is hurting without judgment or advice, pick up some garbage on a walk, put a rogue shopping cart back in its place in the parking lot, ask an elderly person how their day is going, make a special dinner for your spouse who had a hard day, pick up someone for a meeting when you really would rather do something else, say a sincere hello to the clerk at the check-out counter . . .

For Michael, doing all of these "little things" matters now. They are all important to the person he is becoming. And no one needs to know he is doing them . . . just him and God.

Where Do You Stand?

Question 1: In what areas was I selfish during my active addiction? In what areas am I selfish in my recovery?

Question 2: What can I do to become less selfish?

Question 3: What are my special gifts or talents that can be used for service work?

Tool #24

Take it easy
(Introducing peace, calm, smooth patches, and good things in your life)

Classroom Wisdom:

"In the final analysis, the hope of every person is simply peace of mind." —*Dalai Lama*

"For peace of mind we need to resign as general manager of the universe." —*Larry Eisenberg*

"Sometimes I sits and thinks, and sometimes I just sits." —*Satchel Paige*

24. Take it easy
(Introducing peace, calm, smooth patches, and good things in your life)

Tendency:

During our active addictions, our lives were filled with chaos, danger, and overall drama. As we lived in this unpleasant state, day after day, it became our way of life. Hangovers, binges, lost time and money, people screaming at us, crying all around us, anger, lying, self-loathing, remorse, constant fear, etc., etc.

Over time, we learned to accept this type of mire. We knew how we must act and what we must do to survive in it. We got numb to that sick feeling inside of us, the gnawing at our souls, along with the associated fear and remorse. So we engaged in our addictions even more. Our lives and the lives of those around us continued to worsen . . . and we adjusted to the pain and misery by whatever means we could employ.

In recovery, our lives eventually improve. Over the years, I have witnessed countless stories of transformation. Not only for the addict, but like a stone thrown in the water, the healing effect ripples through the lives of family and friends. The change begins on the inside of us, our souls, if you will.

We begin doing things that are constructive, positive, and nurturing. We treat others and ourselves with increasing care. We make amends and clear up the wreckage of our past. We discover who our God is and start building a personal relationship with Him. We learn to take a good look at ourselves on a daily basis and begin the lifetime process of personal growth. As our lives improve, we become less selfish and begin turning our attention, slowly at first, to helping others. All these actions move us toward becoming the person God meant us to be. Along with this "inside job", most of us find that our external lives, health, finances, careers, relationships, etc., improve, sometimes dramatically, as well.

Then a new challenge appears along our recovery path. Slowly or sometimes suddenly, peace, calm, and serenity come over us seemingly out of nowhere. Most of us initially do not even recognize this new condition. This is not surprising based on our chaotic past including, for many of us, our childhood years.

So welcome to the new phase of life where disorder, uncertainty, and fear are minimized, reduced significantly, or even removed at times. Sounds like a positive development, right? Yes; however, there may be a complication. This is all new to us and, as illogical as it may appear, *we do not know how to enjoy all this goodness.* Sounds crazy doesn't it? Well, the truth is we have not yet learned the tools that are geared for these periods of smooth sailing. So what normally happens? We consciously, or otherwise, do things to mess things up again. We instinctively know what type of actions will get us back to the comfort zone of chaos that we know so well, and there we are back in the mire once more.

Recovery Tool:

We will keep repeating this undermining cycle until we learn how to know, understand, accept, and get comfortable with the full and rewarding life that recovery brings us. In other words, we learn to embrace a new, much more positive, equilibrium.

First, we recognize that, through recovery, our inner selves will begin (and continue) to improve over time. For each of us, the improvement has its own shape and form; however, the phrase "goodness" covers it for me. Recognition and acknowledgement of this new condition are important. Just as when we have problems and issues that we share within the recovery community, it's now important that we "report on" the positive changes that are happening to us. Just talking about them aloud will help us accept them as a new part of our world.

Then the most important discovery I made: be careful that when this change happens, we don't get lazy and forgetful and stop doing the action steps that helped us get to this positive state. We focus on our gratitude list that includes God and the people around us. We journal to capture our new discoveries on paper. We continue helping others who are struggling, who are in the same place we started, and share with them the hope of a brighter future. (They may not believe getting there is possible for them, but we must share our hope nevertheless.) We work our total program of recovery, stay vigilant, exert healthy self-discipline, and maintain an attitude of thankfulness. We do our best to remain spiritually connected.

We learn that it is okay, a blessing, actually, not to be living in a state of chaos, but instead enjoy the rewards of periods of peace, calm, and serenity. Isn't this peaceful state of being what we were searching for when we were engaging in our addictions?

Now we know there is a better way, the right way, the spiritual way.

Personal Story:

Michael was new to recovery. His sponsor, Bill, came to spend some time with him at his home. Michael sat for just a second or two on the couch, then went to make some coffee. A minute later he got up to turn the television on. Next he went to open the door to get some fresh air. Then off to put the clothes in the dryer. A few seconds later he was up to check the temperature on the thermostat. Then he wandered over to the front door to make sure it was locked.

After observing Michael for a while, Bill asked the following: "Michael, are you uncomfortable? What's the problem?"

"Yes," Michael said, "not sure what it is."

Bill then instructed Michael, "I want you to try something. Just sit here on this couch and don't move for a while. Don't do anything but sit. Just practice getting comfortable, feeling uncomfortable."

Michael was stunned at the suggestion. Wow, he thought, that is a really scary idea . . .

Many months later, Michael was driving in his car, and from seemingly out of nowhere, a wave of peace and calm came over him. He was momentarily comfortable with himself and the entire world: who he was, where he was, and where he was headed in life. The feelings of peace, calm, and serenity were so strong that Michael began to cry tears of joy. He had to pull his car over to avoid getting in an accident.

As he sat there, he realized he wasn't sure what was happening, so he called Bill. Michael explained the situation, and Bill said, "Just sit there for a while and enjoy the peace, calm, and serenity." This has happened to Michael on several more occasions, but not nearly as many as he would like.

Where Do You Stand?

Question 1: Have I experienced periods of peace, calm, or serenity? Where and when?

Question 2: What do I believe happened for me to receive this gift?

Question 3: What am I doing to obtain or maintain this positive spiritual condition?

Tool #25

Follow the yellow brick road
(Build a vision)

Classroom Wisdom:

"Be somebody you would be proud to know." —Anonymous

"Life isn't about finding yourself. Life is about creating yourself."
—*George Bernard Shaw*

*"If we don't change the direction we are headed, we will end up
where we are going."* —*Chinese Proverb*

25. Follow the yellow brick road
(Build a vision)

Tendency:

As addicts in recovery, we focus considerable effort in taking the actions necessary to avoid relapsing into our addictions. We go to meetings, work the 12 steps, talk to our sponsors, engage in the fellowship, and pursue spiritual growth through many sources. We find and build a relationship with a Power greater than ourselves. We skip going to places where there is temptation, and we stay away from people and things that may trigger relapse. These actions can be classified as defensive measures against relapse, good protective actions and attitudes that have been successful in helping us stay free from addiction. They serve as the cornerstones of recovery.

In addition to freedom from addiction, working all the tools of recovery also enables our growth. This growth is evident in how we view others and ourselves, and how we carry on in all our thoughts and actions. We are in the midst of a major transformation. Our old, addictive selves start to fade away and our new, recovering selves begin to emerge—not unlike the miracle of the journey of the caterpillar to butterfly. The process is slow and not without pain and discomfort. However, the miracle does happen, as we will clearly recognize at some point (and observe in others). Just like the birthing process, we emerge a new person—with new hope and a new future.

Recovery Tool:

In addition to implementing tools against relapse, it is also important that we look beyond the addictions we are eliminating from our lives. We can focus on a future "us" that is emerging from our transformation through recovery. In a sense, we are leaving behind the misguided person we had become through addiction, and moving toward a person we will learn to love and respect.

What would a healthy, non-addictive personality look like? *A person who lets go of anger and resentments? someone who seeks growth over immediate gratification? Who helps others without asking for or expecting anything in return? Who consistently seeks to understand a God of his/her understanding? Who deals with life on life's terms, without escaping, even when things get difficult? Who can be counted on to show up when promised? Who has a healthy and growing self-respect?*

What goals should we have regarding our relationships with others? *A respected father, mother, brother, sister, son, or daughter? Reliable and productive employee? An active member of the recovery community, an involved member of our church of choice, a helpful, contributing member of the human race?*

What type of actions and attitudes would make us feel good about ourselves? *Taking better physical care of ourselves? growing spiritually? helping others in need? having good, clean fun? being tolerant of others?*

To lead a fulfilling life, as opposed to just fighting our addictions, it's important we seek the answer to these and other related questions, i.e., what God would have us do in this life and who He would have us become.

It's important to take time to develop a picture of the "new us". Creating an outline of our life's goals and dreams and then putting it on paper will allow us to evaluate our progress. It doesn't matter where we are starting from. What's of much more importance is understanding where we are headed. We can revisit this vision on a regular basis, tracking progress and making changes as they become evident. Growth will surely lead to addition, expansion, and adjustment of our vision—all in a positive, God-inspired direction.

This movement toward personal lifelong fulfillment, along with our "defensive relapse prevention tools", will serve as a powerful game plan to get us to a place we never thought possible—not just free from the compulsion of addiction, but with a meaningful purpose and a joy of being alive. If we like who we are, or, more precisely, who we are becoming, we will be much less tempted to find ways to escape from ourselves and the lives we are leading.

Personal Story:

Michael recently attended a spiritual retreat where the theme was "Build a vision for your life". Participants were asked to do just that, build a personal vision for where they see themselves headed, now that they have committed to a program of recovery.

Michael wrote the following: I'd like to become a great father, a caring husband, a good friend, a pleasant person to be around, a person committed to recovery from all addictions, a person who trusts in a caring God, someone who takes time to help others and makes this world just a little better place to live . . .

In final reflection, he saw the humor and truth in the following:

I'm not where I want to be, but I know where I'm headed and thank God I'm not where I used to be!

Where Do You Stand?

Question 1: What was the vision for my life while in the midst of my addictions?

Question 2: What is my vision for the new me?

Question 3: What actions do I plan on taking to ensure my vision is fulfilled?

Final Thoughts

MANY OF US SUFFERING from addiction(s) have been shown a way out through the power of a God-inspired recovery. Fortunately, some of us choose this path and begin the climb out of the deep, dark hole that we could not escape from alone. Then, through the grace of God, we have been freed from the compulsion and obsession of our addictions.

Following this incredible release, we come to understand that just abstaining from our addiction is only a beginning. Yes, stopping the thing that is ruining our lives and those around us is a critical and required first step. However, we soon discover that we must find a new set of coping skills to survive and thrive in the world around us. We need a new way to navigate through all that life brings us, good and bad.

To this end, many in recovery have found that "recovery tools" abound. I have done my best to describe 25 of these tools and the practical ways we can implement them into our lives. These spiritual tools have helped change my life as well as the lives of many in recovery. They are simple, but not necessarily easy to incorporate on a lifelong basis. My suggestion is to take them as you need them and begin building your own "recovery tool kit". Pull them out throughout the day as you live life on life's terms. Sharpen them often by engaging in the wide array of recovery activities available to us all. Share them with others, and you will find that day by day they will broaden, deepen, and mature.

My hope and prayers are that this book, and the wisdom it contains, will help and guide you on your own personal journey of recovery. A journey that will be filled with excitement, surprise, promise . . . and a peace not of our own understanding.

Final questions:

Question 1: What tools are most important for me to use to guard against relapse?

Question 2: What additional work do I need to do regarding recovery tools?

Question 3: How may I use this book to help others?

Afterword

S O NOW MY BOOK is finished and with it my feeling that I have
followed God's will to the best of my ability. I have one final
prayer, the same prayer I said the first time I told my story of recovery
before a large group meeting:

If this book helps just *one* person, just *one* addict get better,
then my efforts to write this book and get it published—in fact, in
a broader sense, my whole life in recovery—have truly been directed
and blessed by God.

About the Author

RICK H. HAS BEEN in recovery from alcohol addiction for over 22 years. He is an active member of the 12 step community, sponsoring and mentoring many in recovery. Since 2001, he has organized and co-facilitated spiritual retreats for individuals in recovery and others seeking spiritual growth. He has had over 20 articles on recovery published in recovery periodicals.

Rick and his wife, Susan, live in the Chicagoland area and recently celebrated 25 years of marriage. They have two grown children, Stephanie and Scott.

CPSIA information can be obtained at www.ICGtesting.com
Printed in the USA
LVOW132057201212

312401LV00002B/197/P